All the
Small
Things

CEE RAINEY

Wrate's Publishing

First published 2021 by Wrate's Publishing

ISBN 978-1-8383400-3-2

Copyright © Cee Rainey, 2021
Internal illustrations by Krystal Boyd

Edited and typeset by Wrate's Editing Services
www.wrateseditingservices.co.uk

A CIP catalogue record for this book is available from the British Library.

Contents

THE MOTHERLOAD - (BLOGS FOR MUMMY) - 137

Drawing Your Own Conclusions

Foreword

I was a nanny – and a damn good one, even if I say so myself – for twenty-five years. To prove it, there is a legion of living, breathing humans all over the world whom I have changed, fed and watered. I feel most privileged to have been part of their lives. I've had a hand in raising wee ones from the top to the bottom of the globe, starting in New Zealand, then Australia, before moving onto America, where I managed ski resort crèches, and the UK, where I was a fabled 'London Nanny', hobnobbing around Chelsea, Notting Hill and Chiswick while working for the rich and sometimes famous.

Working with children was my calling. My nearest and dearest always used to remark how good I was around kids; I understand them and seem to instinctively know their wants and needs. Having learned their natural rhythms, I know what comes next with regards to their progress and development, both cognitive and physical. I have dedicated my working life and a lot of my spare time to hanging out with them.

Alongside my professional life, I also carried a deep-seated desire to be a mum myself. In my heart of hearts, I knew that holding one of my own was going to be the icing on the cake. And now, after many years of looking after other people's bundles of joy, I finally got a mini me. But she was so hard fought for. I'm a late bloomer, boomer and breeder. This wasn't my choice, it's just that the stars didn't align for me early on in my life. This means that I am classed as a 'geriatric mother'. This nice term is the medical profession's way of saying old (40-something). With the odds against me falling pregnant becoming seemingly greater with the passing of every month, I rearranged my life, stuck my foot firmly in the closing door of my fertility and took things into my own hands. Or, more to the point, I put things into the highly qualified hands of science.

Having tried and failed to become a mum for twenty years, I was forced to admit I needed a little help. I have endometriosis, which led to my fallopian tubes becoming blocked, but I was assured that all was not lost.

As a single lady, I did what any modern woman would do and reached out for a sperm donor. And I knew exactly who to contact – my first love from twenty years earlier. At the point of our amicable breakup (I wanted to travel, he didn't), he'd made me a promise that could have come straight from the plot of a romcom, 'If you get to forty and you want a baby, get in touch . . .' We had some mutual friends in common, so he wasn't hard to locate on Facebook, and I plucked up the courage to message him and remind him of his promise. Luckily, he answered the call. Well, it was either going to end in a baby or a restraining order. Together, we had a little girl, and the process went so well that my sperm donor also became my husband. I mean, who wouldn't marry the guy who, upon agreeing to have a baby with you, tells you he's going to spend the duration of the pregnancy getting you to fall back in love with him? In fact, it didn't take me long to realise that I had never actually stopped loving him. I relocated from London to Northern Ireland, where he is a single dad of three boys, and we became a noisy, wonderful family of six. Our daughter is the jewel of our family and the glue that holds us together. And wow, she has taught me a thing or two! She has not only reinforced what I knew from being a nanny, but she has shown me so much more about being a parent, and it's this that I now wish to share with you.

Pick'n'Mix

How to use this book:

I've divided the blogs into three sections:

» Milestones (baby's first year)

» Insider Trading (blogs about baby)

» The Motherload (blogs for Mummy)

Now, I want you to imagine each blog as a sweet in a jar. Do you remember how as kids, a special treat was to use our pocket money to buy pick'n'mix? We tried this and loved that, returning for our favourites again and again. I think that parenting is a bit like being in a room full of colourful jars of sweets, only our choices are between tried and tested methods, old wives' tales, new schools of thought, friendly advice and our own intuition. I constructed this book for you to read as you need. Rather than going through it chronologically, go to the blogs that resonate with you, or match the stage either you or your baby are at: it's a dip in/dip out, if you will. So, I want you to take a paper bag and fill it with the sweets (blogs) you are drawn to, then keep doing this throughout your parenting life. Some sweets you will come back to and some you will find didn't taste, feel or look right. Your selection is yours and yours alone, and it's what works for you. No two bags will be the same, just as no two households, babies or families are. This is what makes them so special. Now, dig in.

MILESTONES
(BABY'S FIRST YEAR)

Gums, Tums and Bums - Teething

They're not even out of that newborn stage when suddenly they're in danger of drowning in their own dribble. Yes, teething has started. Their hands, their fists, your hands, in fact, anything they can get hold of to shove into their mouths to relive the pain will do. In our house, it's Daddy's thumb. It's the right size, she can hold onto it and it seems to be the right level of squishy versus hardness. Nightly, he ends up dripping in saliva from the wrist down. We should have taken out shares in a bib company, as the rate at which she saturates them is incredible. And the grizzling when not even Daddy's thumb will do is hard to bear. But if you're going through this, there is help at hand, not only in the form of wonderful teething rings and gel toys they can really chomp on, but in home remedies and over-the-counter soothers to take the edge off.

First off, teething comes in stages:

- » Movement – this causes the tsunami of drool
- » Cutting – the tooth splits the gums
- » Eruption – the tooth pops through

Gums

The first sign of teething is the dribble. This excess of saliva does two things; it either gets swallowed, unbalancing their tummy acid, or it gushes down their face, irritating their chin and neck (and any skin it reaches), so you will need bibs to soak up the excess. If it gets dry around the neck, it can go hard and make any rash worse. They will get red and sore on their chin, from where both of you have been trying to wipe away the river. Vaseline or a cream with an oil base will help to stop the saliva interacting with the skin. I've even used a lip balm all over the chin to act as a barrier. Gently pat away any wetness first, so you are applying it to dry skin. Think of when you have a cold; the more you wipe your nose, the rawer it gets.

Tums

What is not flowing down their chin is being swallowed, which brings on tummy problems. All this excess fluid upsets the natural balance of the stomach, and it will also aggravate any pre-existing conditions. So, if they have reflux or colic, it will get worse. I have found that if you feed babies and burp them in an upright position, it keeps all the fluids where they are supposed to be.

Bums

The excess fluid has to go somewhere, and this in turn causes nappy rash. This can become extremely sore and even burn this sensitive part of the body, which, as you can imagine, is exceptionally painful. So, if you know that bubs has started teething, make sure you slather this area with cream. The thicker the better (mixing Vaseline with any over-the-counter nappy cream will give you the best consistency), as it coats those cheeks and acts as a barrier. Definitely use the thicker variety if you missed the first signs and notice redness on the wee one's buns, as it can and will accelerate quickly into a real pain in the arse.

Another signal that your baby will give you is pulling at their ears, usually the one on the side that hurts the most. And their cheeks get in on the act, too. They go red, sometimes bright red, like they have been slapped, on the side that the teeth are moving. (This is not to be confused with slapped cheek syndrome; with this, bubs will have a significant temperature and be listless and generally unwell.)

Their cheeks will also be hot, but only on the part that's red. If it's the molars coming through, the teething may be accompanied by a slight temperature.

Pain relief is vital for teething; baby's teeth are literally moving and slicing through their gums, and no one should go through this without something to help take the edge off. I use a teething powder that you can buy over the counter and is also homeopathic. (This is widely available in all countries, and it has various names and differing ingredients.) I call it baby crack, as over the years I've seen the kids in my charge light up when they see it, as they know their pain will be going away soon. The bigger kids even used to bring me the sachet to give to them. My baby now is no exception; she wasn't sure the first time round, but now she associates being pain free with this strange powder and opens her mouth ready to receive it. The science bit is that it has a high alkaline content and diffuses the acid in the mouth and stomach.

When my daughter is really bad, I also give her baby ibuprofen and paracetamol. In addition, I use a variety of toys, necklaces (for me and her), food types and touch to help her fight the pain. Here's a rundown.

Toys. There are some really good teething toys on the market. I prefer the gel and silicone ones, as they are extremely chewy. The ones with gel inside can be put in the freezer to provide extra relief.

Necklaces. You can buy fashionable teething necklaces that will go with your outfit and are exactly the right length for bubs to grab and shove into their mouth when you are holding them. These are designed with beads that are just right for little mouths and shaped to give relief to sore gums. (Look online, as there will be someone in your area selling them. Search along the lines of 'silicone baby teething necklace for mum/nursing necklace', etc.) I've found that standard necklaces aren't really conducive to everyday life during this time, as bubs will grab them, get caught up in them and even break them.

I also put an amber necklace on my wee one. It's thought that the natural oils in a baby's skin mix with the gemstone and get reabsorbed to give them a natural, anti-inflammatory boost and pain relief. There is no scientific evidence, but I've sworn by them for twenty-five years.

Food types. Cucumber sticks are great. Think of how beauticians put cucumbers on your eyes at spas to reduce the puffiness and help you look younger, well, the same principle applies for your little one. Although babies have skin that people pay good money for, the swelling in their gums can be relieved by the vegetable, especially if it's frozen. As the water content is high, it easily turns to ice. The relief of cold cucumber on hot, swollen gums is a godsend to little ones. Plus, when their actual teeth do come through and they are moving onto solids, cucumber provides one of their five a day, so it's good to get them used to the taste. Pita bread is also helpful, as it's chewy and it takes a bit of work to bite through. There are also over-the-counter foods (but check the sugar content), such as soft biscuits, rice crackers or a harder biscuit called a rusk, although the latter two can also be made at home.

Reflexology and **baby massage.** As explained earlier, teething baby's tummies can fill up with excess fluids that travel up and down through their system. As well as getting colic/reflux, they may also become constipated, or, at the other end of the scale, suffer bouts of diarrhoea. There are many good techniques to combat this. You might be able to sign up to a baby massage course in your area, where you can learn the best way to help with your wee one's digestion. You'll be taught how to assist in moving blockages in the gut and how to help the bowel cope with the influx of acids, etc. Reflexology is also a wonderful way to help bubs relax and target the areas affected by teething pains. For example, there are specific parts of the foot that you can press to alleviate pain in the gums. Do look it up online or find a practitioner to help you. In the meantime, you could try just gently massaging their whole foot, from toe to heel and back up again, while singing, *This Little Piggy*.

Just remember that you survived this phase in your life unscathed, and your baby will, too, even though, boy, will they complain about it! And it can be hard to hear, to watch and to experience it alongside them. Hopefully, some of these tricks of the trade and tried and true ways to sidestep the pain of teething will work for your little one.

Tummy Time

When you hear the fuss babies make over this, you could be forgiven for thinking it was 'Torture Time'. You pop them down for a second and they complain, "I don't like this, pick me up!" But this is good. "Why?" I hear you ask. Well, frustration is your friend and the key to making their brain work. It motivates them to move and lifts and propels them, literally, to the next level. Firstly, it encourages them to bring their heads up, even if it's only to eyeball you and make you feel guilty for putting them there. Secondly, it will embolden them to start rolling and, eventually, crawling. But boy, will they complain about doing it, and I know how hard that is to listen to. They will get louder when you don't react, but you must stick to your guns. This is your first lesson in the 'Mum knows best' and 'You're just going to have to trust me' moments. Start small, with a couple of minutes three or four times a day, working up to longer sessions until they actually want to be on their tummies. Yes, that moment will come. Once they realise that it leads to independence, they love it.

For your own peace of mind, here is why it's good and why you know best.

» It's great for digestion, as the pressure on their tummies will help to push things along, shall we say, so expect a poop afterwards.

» It's beneficial for building their head and neck strength and their control. I popped my little one on a doughnut cushion to begin with, so she could lean on her hands and get her legs kicking. This led to her wanting to move, and also meant she wasn't flat on her face.

» It kickstarts their cognitive development and motor skills. As they start to reach out for things, their hand-eye coordination will improve.

» It's wonderful for recognition skills, as the smile on their face when they raise their head and see you smiling back at them is wonderful. It really helps them to focus their eyes and movements, thus maintaining the connection.

When they have had enough, I roll them over. But before you know it, they will be raising themselves up, as if doing a mini push-up, as they look around for you. They will also reach out for toys that catch their eye. And expect to see them rolling over all over the shop, and becoming lodged under furniture. It is wonderful to watch them make the physical and mental connections and use muscle memory and control to move in their desired direction. I get down on the floor and lie with my daughter, maintaining eye contact and talking to her. By engaging (distracting) her this way, she fully gets the benefit of floor play. Being down there with her to begin with helps to increase the time on her tummy. So she has something to look at, I pop flat books and a colourful blanket underneath her. And if she is interested in doing her own thing, that gives me five minutes to put on the kettle or go to the loo. There are many aids you can use, for example:

Blow up doughnut rings with a material outer layer and activities sewn into it.

Semi-circular breastfeeding pillows that will double up as back support cushions later on, when they are sitting.

Activity mats that have mobile hanging attachments, as well as sensory play corners and textured pads sewn into them.

Chew toys or **toys that crinkle or squeak**. **Brightly coloured soft toys** that you can scatter around.

Saying all that, what my daughter wanted most during Tummy Time was the remote and my wallet and car keys!

When they get the hang of it, they'll become excited whenever they're on their tummy and start flailing their legs and arms. They will roll over and play by reaching for any items that you have hung over them. In turn, this is wonderful for cross patterning (the synapses in the left and right sides of the brain), which is imperative for cognitive development and gross motor skills. What this means, in layman's terms, is that the left brain controls the right side, and vice versa, so when you cross the centre line, i.e., touch opposite toes and fingers to each other, or they 'march' in a baby way (opposite legs and arms going), it switches on the different sides of their brain and motivates them to get mobile. They'll start to lift their head, commanding control over it (which is easier said than done), before coordinating their limbs and weight distribution to roll over. Next, they'll push up their torso and lurch forward, finally getting their knees up and rocking to and fro. Then comes the funny part, as when they eventually do get lift off and crawl, they'll go backwards. Again, you'll find them wedged under furniture, but they will get the hang of it and find first gear.

All this happens because of Tummy Time, so pop your earplugs in and display your finest 'Mummy knows best' grimace, ignoring (for a short time) all the complaints of mistreatment directed at you from your baby. Some significant stepping stones and milestones are at play.

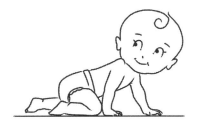

Head, Shoulders, Knees and Toes

My wee one is about to roll and, as exciting as that may be, finding her wedged under the sofa and suddenly seeing all the potential baby hazards in my house and all the baby proofing I need to embark upon got me thinking. People keep saying, "Ooh, she'll be crawling in no time," and it's clear there is a natural order to things. The way I remember it is via that old nursery rhyme, *Head, Shoulders, Knees and Toes.*

» **Head** – getting control of their body

   This is what bubs needs to gain control of first. They'll do this by lifting their head, which will strengthen their neck, and through looking from side to side.

» **Shoulders** – tummy time

   By using their arms and shoulders to push themselves up (essentially doing a push up from the waist up), bubs will learn to twist their body, and even roll over.

» **Knees** – crawling

   Bringing their knees up underneath them and using their stronger shoulders and arms to raise their torso will eventually lead to them crawling.

» **Toes** – standing and walking

Once they have mastered the art of crawling, there will be no stopping them. They will reach the walls and furniture and immediately want to know what's up there, pulling themselves up on their toes. This will help them to learn balance and direction.

There is a flow to the song (which you now won't be able to get out of your head, I apologise) and a natural progression that the body and brain follow in getting up and running. There is also that old saying that you have to crawl before you stand, stand before you walk and walk before you run. All things in good time and in the right order.

So, here's how I see it. First comes the head holding, which involves getting control of their necks. If you think how big their heads are in relation to their bodies, this is a major feat! Then they'll begin looking around and tracking you, first by smell, then by sound and then by sight. Once they have mastered all this and accepted tummy time (they will hate it to begin with but stick with it, as it's so helpful in muscle development in the head, neck and shoulders, as well as in cognitive development and motor skills for arm and leg movement), you will see them trying to roll. It's wonderful to watch. They'll try and balance their legs and arms to push off from, and to get all the right weights and counters in place to go over.

Once they get the hang of it, they are off and rolling around on the floor like no one's business, all the while looking rather proud of themselves and smug. But soon this won't be enough, as their brain will say, "Up, up and away", and they'll be wiggling like a worm across the floor with their bums in the air and their arms flailing, which will soon translate into the next step of crawling. As I said, their cognitive development and gross motor skills will harmonise to get their arms to push up, their knees to bend and their bums to rise and move in one formation. This usually happens in reverse, and I don't mean they get it all wrong, I mean they literally go backwards, usually wedging themselves once again under the sofa and looking for assistance. But they will get it. Now, here is the disclaimer and my own thinking and training from being a childcare professional for twenty-five years. If your child commando crawls (just the arms), spider walks (up on their hands and feet vs palms and knees), doesn't use opposites (as in left moving with right, and vice versa) or sits up and bum shuffles along (kinda bouncing themselves along the carpet), then get them to stop. I'm sorry if this is controversial, but I totally stand by it. You need to intervene and show them how to crawl. This is to help the synapses of the brain form correct pathways, such as the left-hand side of the body being controlled by the right hand, and vice versa. Crawling left-right, left-right and having the opposite arm and leg combination allows the two sides of the brain to be 'switched on'. This is essential to further development in the brain and has been linked to forming words, reading and writing, coordination and, in some studies, even preventing dyslexia.

You may now be wondering how to do this. Well, take your little one back a step, pop them back on the floor and show them by crossing their centre line with their arms and legs. The centre line, as it says on the tin, runs straight down your body. So, if you touch, say, the toes of their right foot to their left earlobe or bring their left hand to their right knee, this will do the switching on for them and encourage them to crawl. When they are on their tummies, lift them gently and encourage them to rock on their knees to get a forward motion. Put a circle of bribes in front of them, which are just out of reach. This will encourage them to propel themselves forward to get to them. Most of all, get on the floor with them and show them how you crawl!

Around the same time, they will learn to sit. This stepping stone is one that runs alongside crawling. Some babies will learn to sit up first then to lean forward and go into crawling, while others will crawl before leaning back and plopping onto their bums. Sitting and supporting themselves completely is also a feat in itself, as they have to coordinate their heads (very heavy) and spine and bend their knees and arms to balance. As soon as they get it, they will start reaching for things to pick up. There will be a lot of drunken sailor moves and toppling over sideways, and they will need all the help they can get to achieve a soft landing. However, be careful not to help them too much, as they need to learn to balance and first will need the muscle strength. If you help them too much, they may get a false sense of security and hurt themselves, when they think they can when really they can't. Sitting is also a great skill, as the next stepping stone is pulling themselves up. This too is fraught with failure, so it's important for them to be able to plop back onto their bums and be stable.

Life gets interesting when they master the ability to pull themselves up. As a crawler, they can get to places, but until they can figure out how to lift themselves, you just need to baby proof to a certain level, e.g., corners and making sure there is nothing on the floor they can swallow. But when they realise they can go up, well, think of the dinosaur in *Jurassic Park* rising up to the top of the tree. Yes, they can get into everything. Think of their height and then their reach, then add curiosity and the idea to combine reaching up and crawling vertically . . . yes, that's climbing! Anyway, back to pulling up. They will do it to anything that can hold their weight and everything that can't. You will spend many an hour hunched over with your fingers being clung to as they pull themselves up. They have been planking all this time during tummy time, so their core strength is amazing. Trust me, it puts us all to shame. So, inside, it's time to batten down the hatches. Only have things around that they can safely pull up on, such as the coffee table, the sofa and that chair leg. Secure them by ensuring there are no overhanging tablecloths or anything else loose that can be pulled down. There have been many an accident with dressers and drawers coming down on bubs as they pull or climb. Provide them with toys that they can pull themselves up on. A great one is a wooden trolley with heavy blocks in it. It will take their weight well, and once they are stronger, they can push it around as they learn to walk. Plastic ones are good but they're not as stable. I'm not a great advocate of walkers (the round play stations on wheels), as I feel they give them a false sense of balance, and I prefer the school-of-hard-knocks approach, with lots of trial and error.

This totters me nicely into walking. Firstly, they'll want to walk everywhere holding onto your hands. Your back will not forgive you, as you'll be hunched over to accommodate them. They never seem to tire of this new trick/skill. Secondly, when they finally get it, those tentative first steps are wonderful, wobbling and exciting. And that's just you when you have let go of their hands and are walking backwards yelling to anyone who will listen, 'Watch, they're going to go, get the camera!' But seriously, the simultaneous look of determination and fear on their face is great. As a rule of thumb, I have found that once they let go of whatever they are holding onto, be it yourself or a coffee table, and they stand for a second before lowering themselves to a squat and coming back up again, you have just days until they are toddling about the place and you are chasing them around the house to get their pjs on after their bath. Those first couple of weeks of walking are such a wonderful time, as they are literally finding their feet and taking those baby steps. It's beautiful to observe them coming on in confidence and self-awareness.

And then the work really starts! They are off and their confidence has been found and is building all the time. They will now start climbing on anything they can. Bookcases are a favourite, as they're like a ladder. So, do secure all the big items to the wall. The best one is their cot. They will climb in and, best of all, climb out, so maybe think about lowering the sides and/or putting a mattress underneath it for safety.

One other point I want to make and probably should have said a lot further up is this: there are no time limits on these milestones. Your baby will reach them in their own time, and you shouldn't compare them with others, even if they are roughly the same age. I looked after two girls and one walked at ten months but didn't say a word until they were over a year. The other, who was six weeks younger, could speak in full sentences but didn't walk until she was eighteen months. Even if we don't admit it, we tend to compare and contrast our kids with others. It's for either competition – my child is better developed, etc. – or for comfort – oh good, so and so is rolling, my wee one is too, so that's normal. But it's when you start thinking your child is behind or not doing what is normal that you start to question yourself, and them. DON'T! As I said, all in good time. Maybe panic after a couple of years if they still aren't making any significant progress. DO remember to enjoy every bit of this journey with your child. They do so much in the first couple of years and it's a whirlwind. So, take time to breathe and remember to take lots of photos.

Lazy Baby Weaning

'Tis that moment in a baby and mother's life when it's time to feed them solid food, and boy, is it everywhere: on me, on her, on the floor, on the highchair, on her bib, spoon, bowl and on the table legs. I'm not sure how she managed to get it on the latter, but she did, and we are only a week in. You see, I am treading the tightrope between the schools of thought regarding purees and the newly coined Baby-Led Weaning (BLW). As a nanny, I hate that term, as we have been doing it for eons and not calling it anything in particular. And then some smartarse comes along and writes down what we are doing and coins the term, and coins it literally, as there are books and money being made about what we have been practising the whole time. Vent over . . . I could have made a mint!! Nope, I'll stop now!

The theory behind BLW is that you feed your child what you are having, just a softer version, and let them explore new tastes and textures themselves. There is no steaming and batch cooking, no purees in jars and feeding them with a spoon. Rather, you give them squished up this and that, and there needn't be a food processor in sight. They eat what you do, so you're not making different meals, etc. You just cook the food for a little bit longer after you have taken yours out, e.g., the veggies. Just cut up whatever solids you are having into non-chokeable pieces. They need to be manageable chunks for the wee one to hold in their hands and put into their own mouth.

I have practised both the aforementioned schools of thought; pureed and steamed so much that the kitchen resembled a Chinese laundry, and then rebelled, giving my wee ones whatever I was having and finding it went down fine as finger food. I've done this so much I decided to meet the world halfway with *Lazy Baby Led Weaning* (LBLW), which is a term *I've* coined (still hoping to get that book deal!). LBLW treads between the two, as in the baby gets a spoon for things that hands can't grasp, e.g., yoghurts and porridge, baby rice, etc. It gets flavoured with half a squished piece of fruit, uncooked. Then I serve steamed veg that is cut into sticks and small pieces, so she can experiment. Broccoli florets and carrot sticks are good for this. She's also served some of whatever we are having cut up, be that pasta, cottage pie, fish and her favourite, roast chicken, which is all broken up into smaller bits that she then gums to death while we watch her like a hawk in case she starts choking. P.S. if you are going to follow this path then find out about choking vs gagging, as they are different, and one can lead to the other if bubs is interfered with. There are many great visual references on the internet that highlight the differences.

The path I have chosen works for me, my baby and my family. My suggestion is to read up on the various schools of thought, talk to other mums and make your own meals based on what you've learned. They can be tailored exactly to your baby's tastes, your diet and/or any allergies that are in the family. Everyone's experience is different, so rest assured that whatever you choose to do will be right for you and your baby. Bon appetite x

Solids, and NOT the Oral Kind

My little one has gone onto solids, which, in turn, is causing her bowels to produce solids, which is good, though the transition did not pass easily, if you get my drift.

The upside of solids is that your baby is growing up, moving into the next stage of their life, joining the family at mealtimes and in social interactions. Whichever method you choose, be it Baby Led Weaning by the book, Lazy Baby Led Weaning using my tips, or puree based and then moving onto solids, seeing them chew up and swallow real food is wonderful and sad at the same time.

The downside of solids is that your wee one is not a baby anymore. They are no longer dependent on you or a bottle and, in turn, they are becoming more childlike, which leads to more childlike functions, such as sitting up and feeding themselves (or trying to) and more child/adult-like bodily functions, which is the focus of this blog.

Of course, moving onto solids changes the digestive system, and boy, can that create some side effects, wind, for one, and either pebbles for poos or extreme constipation. Just know that this is all a stage and that it will pass (literally). It is a transition for all of you, both inside and out. My daughter went from the extreme of producing dirty nappies in between every change to not going for a week and producing something extremely solid. In the beginning, she had a hard time passing it. We are now into week three of solids (at both ends) and it's starting to pan out.

All the mums I have chatted with about this stage remember the nappy changes, so to speak. It is amazing when your little one does their first solid poo, as it's almost as if they've suddenly become an adult. No longer are we worried about colour and consistency, now it's all about texture and how grown up it is!

But there are ways to help your baby through this 'passing' phase.

Baby Massage. Look it up, learn it and/or go to a class. This is the most wonderful way to help soothe wee tummies and release tensions. It is also a delightful way to spend a few minutes bonding with your baby. There are tummy pressure exercises and leg cycling movements, as well as songs to help you remember the actions and cool names to teach you to do them correctly. These include 'waterfall', 'sun', 'moon' and 'spider walk'. You'll learn to start all the actions over the right side of the baby's stomach and apply pressure to move blockages to their left, where the gut meets the bowel.

Reflexology. Like massage, there are pressure points on the baby's body, especially on their feet, that help relieve physical blockages elsewhere. To find out where these are, you can look them up online or take classes, but if you just rub your baby's feet from their heel to their toe you will hit them all.

Drinks. Gripe water is good for wind and boiled prune juice, along with any other fruit juices, will help to shift blockages, just remember to dilute anything you give to your baby, as fruit juice is full of natural sugars that will risk the development of a sweet tooth.

Tummy time. This is a natural way to encourage the expulsion of gases and the movement of food stuffs. Put them on a pregnancy ball and roll them gently up and down, or pop them on a cushion and/or towel and let them kick it out.

Take it easy on some foods. Some are stodgy and will take a while to move through the gut, especially when digesting them is new. Rice (baby rice), cereals (baby muesli), potatoes, cheese, bananas and pasta can block bums up and take a bit of help getting out. During Lazy Baby Weaning, I discovered that my wee one loves all of these, so I couple them with the 'P' foods that also help them to poop. These include prunes, peaches, peas, pears and plums. Also, blueberries seem to do the trick, as does yoghurt.

Just as we do for ourselves, we need to balance out bub's food intake and make sure they are getting all the right things in the right amounts. And just as we do when it comes to our own diet, we can sometimes misjudge it and end up having trouble at the other end. However, with touch, drinks and a balanced diet, all can be alleviated. Just be ready, as with child poops comes adult smells, and there is no remedy for them, bar maybe a nose peg.

Give Them a Spoon

I'm a bit late to the party when it comes to providing my child with a spoon to feed herself with, which is partly due to laziness on my part – I like feeding her – and partly laziness on her part, as she likes getting fed! Another excuse is that we're doing BLW (Baby Led Weaning), so ninety per cent of what she eats has been finger food, and she's doing great with that. But she's seen us with a spoon and with cutlery, and she wants in.

Spoonfuls of yoghurt are getting snatched away and the communication from her is letting me know she wants to do it herself. She is pointing and grabbing at cutlery, and she is so happy when she gets a set. She is attempting – and at times succeeding – to feed herself. It really is a *see-do* desire to join in, which is similar to when they want to eat whatever you're having. I have to say, I have capitalised on that. As part of the BLW, she got what we were having in cut-up form. However, she now wants to eat just as we do. Her hand-eye coordination is kicking in and she's feeling a great sense of achievement. It's wonderful, but how do you transition from feeding them from the spoon to them doing it themselves?

Well, for one, not quickly or cleanly, so give up the idea that this is in any way going to be a pristine transaction. It's going to be messy and missy, as in for a while they will miss more than they get in. Here is one way I have found for moving from you doing it to, *"I do it!"*

Give them something easy to begin with. It's a no brainer – you're not going to start with peas or fiddly stuff. Start with yoghurt and liquidy things. Porridge/breakfasts are a great place for that. Give them more than they will eat, as there will be a lot of wastage. Batten down the hatches, cover the floor with plastic, and off you go. Give them lots of praise to begin with. Even when they don't get it in, let them know that they are still doing great.

As you want them to actually get food into their stomachs and not go hungry (and as far as I know, nutrients aren't transferred through osmosis), I've found remembering and using the Ps is helpful:

» **Patience**

   They are going to get frustrated and so are you, but as long as you don't appear to be too fussed, they will continue to keep trying.

» **Persevere**

If it looks like it's not going well, don't give up – you guys have got this. Just wait until that lightbulb moment when they do get it, and the sense of accomplishment will be a real confidence boost for both of you.

» **Parental assistance**

The coordination – getting spoon to bowl and food to mouth and back again – is hard. So, help as much as you can. Tilt the bowl. Get one that sticks to the table or tray, so it doesn't move or get flung in frustration. Pop the food on the spoon and hand it to your wee one to pop into their mouth. A little helping hand to begin with is great while they get the hang of it.

» **Pairs**

I find that in the beginning, it's best to give them the spoon as they request it, but have a spare nearby, so they do a mouthful (or cheek or ear, etc.) and you can do a proper mouthful. This way, even if they do get it wrong, they will still get some food in. I find they get less frustrated if they feel like they have control and a spoon in their hand. Even if they are not actually feeding themselves, it calms the situation and eases your fears that they aren't getting enough to eat.

I'm a huge advocate of eating with our little ones, especially with BLW. I hate it when I see kids eating alone in their highchair. Your child needs you, as eating is social, and they will want to mimic your behaviour. Don't just stick them in front of a TV or give them a screen. They need to be part of the interaction that happens at mealtimes, as it's part of the rhythm of family life. They need to eat their food as you would and see you eating up all your vegetables.

They need to see how to hold the cutlery, to twist it, balance it, and use it together to gather the food. The whole point of mealtime is a learning curve for them.

I touched on this before, but the lightbulb moment they will get during this next phase in their development is wonderful. It's a great triumph for them and a hugely proud moment for you. Once they get the hang of it, the mess and the clean-up operation afterwards will lessen, and you'll be able to eat your own food while it's still hot! The boost for their cognitive development in hand-eye coordination will help them get the hang of other skills in the future more easily. The confidence they will feel about being a 'big person' now will be great for their standing in the family, especially when new ones arrive! Having them be able to eat unaided will also open up your menu choices and you'll be able to start going out for dinner, as you are not so reliant on baby food. You can go to restaurants and teach them social graces and how to behave in public. As they leave their baby stage, the world will open up.

So, don't be afraid; get down and dirty and allow them to explore and discover food. There will be a transition period where everything, including them, you, the floor, wall and cat will be covered with that day's culinary choice, but it's part of growing up! If they are ready and telling you, then give them a spoon.

Bag of bugs

Jags, jabs, shots, immunisations, inoculations. . . whatever you call them, they are painful and there will be tears, and that's just you! As horrible as they are, they are part and parcel of the early years of a child's life. Some people feel children are given too many too soon, but this blog is not a debate on the injections and their contents, but more of an acknowledgement that if you go ahead with them for your little one, they can be hard on everyone, with the addition of some advice on the best way to deal with the aftermath.

Firstly, there is the accusing looks you'll receive from bubs concerning why you are letting this person stab them. Then there is the bleeding. For something so little, there is a lot of blood. And when I say little, I don't mean your baby. What I mean is that those tiny needles have a huge impact. The bump, welt and bruise they leave is horrific. Then there is the administering of a pain killer (please seek medical advice over which type to give) and holding your breath for those few minutes in the waiting room to see if they are going to react. For first timers, this can be traumatic.

I have been lucky in that my wee one seems to get over her jabs pretty fast, but I think that's because I am not a first timer and so I am pretty relaxed about the whole thing. It is a necessary evil, it's over pretty quickly and lots of cuddles seem to do the trick. Plus, in my twenty-five years of being a childcare professional, I have seen what not having a shot looks like, a) because there wasn't a vaccine available (the chicken pox one is relatively new) or b) the child got the illness before getting the jab or the parents chose not to get them vaccinated. A quick prick in the leg is better than a week or so of really ill, spotty or swollen children. And that is the best-case scenario. But as I said, I am not here to discuss whether to have shots or not, I am here to offer help for when they do get them and feel like crap afterwards. So, for the puncture site, Arnica, Arnica, Arnica. It's cold to go on and soothes the redness and heat that the jab produces; it also prevents bruising and aids healing.

Painkillers, or whatever quick-acting medication you want to use, are certainly advisable. Following the jab, their body will be a bag of bugs, so any comfort you can provide will be welcomed. There is conflicting advice on when to give the medication; just before the jab (people worry it may mask a temperature, if one develops) or just after, allowing you time to see if a reaction develops. I have always gone with having the relief on hand and administering it in the waiting room directly after the jab. The medication for children is often so full of sugar and is so easy to take that it provides a welcome distraction from the trauma that you have just inflicted on them . . . they still haven't forgiven you, yet.

We all like to comfort eat, especially if we aren't feeling good, so have a bottle or a boob available and offer them as much as they need. On immunisation days, all routines and timings should go out the window, and it should be all about comfort. I have found they will either go off their food at some point or cluster feed as if they are starving. Every child has a different reaction, sometimes to each set of immunisations. I have a friend whose child was OK for the first couple of sets and then on the final booster ended up with blood in her stool, as her stomach reacted so badly to the oral immunisation. If they are feeling off, try to get some water into them, even if it is just from a spoon. Keeping them hydrated will help their recovery.

Cuddles and snuggles are extremely important. This is likely to be the first time your child will experience being ill and not feeling good, and they will need you on hand to reassure them. One way I have found to help regulate their temperature and aid their digestion (as I said, one immunisation is oral) is to go back to basics with skin on skin. It works wonders, both for you and them. Remember that you will be feeling a little fragile yourself, as even though you are actively putting your baby through this for their own good, it's not fun to watch. I suggest indulging in a duvet day afterwards, as both of you will need to take it easy. Let them sleep as much as they want to (this is very useful for later on, too, as a child's body heals in sleep, so when they are sick, just let them rest). As I said earlier, let them eat when and where they want to. Whisper to them gently or sing to them – they'll find your voice reassuring. Just take it slow.

Be ready for the other end. Immunisation messes with their bodies, so it all has to come out somewhere, and it seems to be through their poos. Wow, they can seem never ending and they are sticky and can be runny. The procedure really seems to mess with their poor tummies. So, be ready to change a few bad nappies and have the cream on hand to soothe the savage rash that can come from an upset tum. In the beginning, don't make plans around the days after the immunisation, as you don't want to be changing those nappies in public. Plus, your little one isn't feeling good, so no classes or swimming or racing them around. The after-effects can last up to a week and run into the nights, too. Just stay in and become a jab hermit. Other mums will completely understand!

I hope I am not making this all sound too awful. It's not, it's just not a pleasant time, and I think if you know that then you can prepare and get through it better. Just have the pain meds ready, hoard nappies and wipes (I'm doing cloth nappies and washable wipes, just putting that out there!) and be ready to slather their bum in cream. Clear both your schedules, stock up on favourite foods/snacks (theirs and yours) and batten down the hatches for a few days.

They will hate you for a second and then need you completely for a couple of days. They will be clingy and grizzly and not themselves, but this will pass, and you can feel safe in the knowledge that they are immune to some nasties, and also that they won't remember any of it.

INSIDER TRADING
(BLOGS ABOUT BABY)

Nursery Needs and Wants

Even before bubs has arrived, preparing the nursery is one of the best things you can do for getting in the right mindset for motherhood. Start off by getting some wee things here and there completed; then, as the big day approaches, it's time to think about the bigger picture (the one that's in your head, we all have that perfect image). If you've been thrown a baby shower or have put together a baby registry (much like a wedding present list, this is where you pick out items for people to gift you), then you can start putting the items you've been given in their place. I was lucky – and I'm sure you'll find this too – as when the news got out about my mother-to-be status, the other parents I knew took the opportunity to empty their lofts, basements and garages of all their preloved baby items that they'd been keeping in storage. So, you will hopefully find no shortage of items for your nursery.

Aside from clothes, which are a personal preference, I thought I would give you a list of items that over the years I have found useful. I have many years of experience with setting up and stocking nurseries. While it's nice to have all the gear, some items are a want rather than a need.

Bigger items

Cot. This is an obvious one, but there are so many to choose from. You need to look at what space you have, and your budget. Ideally, they will be in with you for up to six months, so maybe beg, steal or borrow a moses basket or a smaller crib for the early days, something that fits in with your room. You can get some great bedside cribs, which allow them to nestle in next to your bed, so you can bottle or breastfeed them with ease. Or get a 'forever' cot; it will be too large to begin with, and bubs will be dwarfed by it, but the sides can be lowered for feeding (meaning you don't have to lift them out of the cot) and then, when they are bigger, it can be transferred to their room with the sides up. Finally, the sides can be removed to make their first bed.

A dressing table that doubles up as a changing table. This is a handy piece of furniture, and if you buy wisely, it can last a lifetime. Make sure the top is at waist height for you, as after numerous botty changes, bending down will hurt. It needs to be long and wide enough to accommodate the change mat, a basket of nappies, wipes and all the lotions and potions that a new baby requires. My advice is to get one with drawers, instead of having open shelves, etc., as you can then keep your spares of the aforementioned items in them. Plus, when they're crawling around and curious, bubs won't be able to climb up the drawers and pull things down.

Rocking chair or comfy chair. On those lazy nights when you get to rock them to sleep, it's good to have a comfortable, supportive chair to relax in. A footrest is optional.

Smaller items

Laundry hamper. Remember that you'll be doing a zillion changes of clothes.

Nappy bucket. If you're going with cloth nappies, then this is invaluable. Get one with a net laundry insert for ease of washing. If you're going with disposables, you can either get a rubbish bin or a specialist nappy bin.

Monitor. There are some fancy ones out there that you can connect to your phone. They come with portable screens and two-way speakers, so you can listen in and talk to your baby, or even just listen to music. It doesn't matter what the model is, just get one, as they take the guess work out of being there for them when they wake up.

Changing stations. You will need two of everything, as no matter how regimented you expect to be, you'll end up changing them in the living room during the day. So, get two changing mats and two baskets stocked up with all their lotions, potions, wipes and nappies.

Tiny things

Face flannels, nail clippers, thermometer, snot sucker (AKA a nasal aspirator, this plastic tube, which helps to clear blocked noses, will prove invaluable, trust me), **oils** for baby massage and your chosen brand of **bottom cream.**

Bathroom items

Fluffy hooded towels.

Bath toys. Choose from rubber ducks or foam letters, they're always lots of fun.

Bath insert. My personal preference is a flannel/mesh one that fits on a metal frame, but there are plastic versions, as well as whole baths that fit inside your existing one. You can also get foam inserts that will fit into your kitchen or bathroom sink.

Lotions and **potions** for keeping their skin baby soft. Special soaps and shampoos, hairbrushes and combs.

Optional extras

Bookcase. You will be the recipient of lots of keepsakes and trinkets, as well as books for now and as they grow, so if you can fit a bookcase in, it'll be a good investment, providing storage for now and a library for later.

Nightlight. These come in all shapes and sizes, in toy form, with music and/or a dimmer switch. You can even make them yourself (I filled a cider jar with fairy lights). They can bring calm to the room and prevent you from stubbing your toe on your way in and out at night.

Plants. It's always good to have something living in with bubs, as it cleanses the air and adds a nice touch to the room.

Wardrobe. They will need one eventually, but this is one of those items that can be left out of the nursery for now.

Feeding Pillow. I swear by these crescent-shaped wraparound pillows. At the beginning, when they're tiny, it's natural to think a standard pillow will be fine, but bubs is going to get bigger and heavier and when this time comes, especially during the night feeds, you'll need something more supportive. Trust me, your back will thank you. Plus, these pillows are great for tummy time training and for when they're practising how to sit up.

Wall friezes or **pictures.** Babies of all ages love having things to look at. It's been proven that newborns respond to black and white, though as they get older, they will be able to make out blocks of solid colour and simple shapes. At this point, you can fill their room with your chosen theme, be that a particular colour scheme, or, for example, Disney, Winnie the Pooh or jungle animals. Just have some fun.

Storage bins. For toys, bath things, towels, sheets, sleep bags, muslins and blankets. You get the gist.

Blackout curtains or **blinds.** These are useful for helping babies differentiate between daylight, light naps and night-time.

Must haves for outside the nursery

Pushchair. As there are so many options, I will leave this one up to you. I have gone with a Maclaren with a bassinet insert. It will grow with my baby's needs and age. But you could go high end with something like a Bugaboo or spend less by shopping at a local baby store or charity shop. There is nothing wrong with preloved. Whatever you decide, make sure it fits your own needs, be that having somewhere to put your coffee and multiple shopping bags or being easy to fold with one hand so you can get it into the car easily. Personally, I'd go for a model that had ample storage underneath or behind and a rain cover and a zip up footmuff for the winter months. It should also have space for a buggy board, for if you want one later, and be adjustable to fit your partner's height. The wheels should be lockable, with good brakes, and I'd pick one with a hood to keep the sun off. Finally, make sure it's easy to put into flat mode.

Before bubs arrives, it's essential to practise putting the pushchair up and down. Do this several times, both in and out of the house. Make sure you have all the bits pushed in and down, so that it doesn't collapse on bubs, and that you can fold it in a hurry if you need to.

Car seat. These are essential, unless, of course, you don't own a car. These days, they aren't expensive and there are a variety of options. You can get ones that will last for six years, as they transform into a booster seat as your child gets older. There are ones that swivel on their base to allow side access into the car and ones that can be transferred with ease from the car to a pushchair. Some can be secured in place using a seatbelt and others with ISOFIX, an internationally standardised car seat fitting system (most new/newish cars come with ISOFIX bars already fitted in the backseat, which is something to think about when buying a new family vehicle). Get advice from friends, family and the shop assistant, and ask the latter to help you fit it correctly. Also, get a mirror that you can fix to the backseat headrest and swivel, allowing you to see what your wee one is up to while they are back facing.

Playmats. As much as you can never get in enough cuddles with bubs, there are times when you will need to pop them down for a minute, even if it is just so you can go to the loo. This is when you need a soft, interactive playmat. There are so many on the market, but I advise getting one that has a hanging bar with interactive toys on it, both soft and furry, a mirror and something for them to coo at and reach for. Make sure it's machine washable and that the toys are detachable, as some will have electronics in their tummies that could malfunction, especially if they come into contact with water. I've witnessed a mum with a hammer smashing small toys that wouldn't switch off. It was like a scene from a horror movie.

Slings and/or **front packs.** These allow you to free up your hands while carrying bubs. Many areas have a sling/front pack library, where you can try them out and get to grips with putting them on. You can go from feeling like you're handling a bondage harness to performing baby origami in one afternoon! I have a small frame, so front packs are too long in the body for me and I end up with bubs around my navel and sore shoulders. Instead, I wear a sling, which can be tied in different ways, meaning I can carry bubs sideways or upright, facing in or out, snuggling right up to me or sitting on my hip (this one is only for toddlers). Do try before you buy.

Setting up the room

Be it your room or theirs, make it airy and light. This may be a stark contrast to the dark and warm womb, but fresh air and light is so important for them and their skin. Having natural light pouring into the room will get their Vitamin D levels up, and it's a wonderful, natural way of boosting their immunity. Plants and/or a salt lamp will naturally purify the air and help them to relax. Don't put them too close to a radiator or where they'll be in direct sunlight.

It is truly overwhelming to think that someone so small needs so much. But trust me, you will get more stuff than you need, so if you want to pare it down to the basics, then stick to my list. Find your style, while you get a say in how their room is decorated, and then accept gifts and hand-me-downs and shop to your heart's content.

Hi Ho, hi ho, it's off to Hospital we Go

However mentally prepared you may be, the act of actually turning up at the hospital to give birth can be daunting, especially if it's your baby letting you know that it's time, and you don't feel quite ready. In speaking to other soon-to-be mums and from my own experience, maintaining some sort of control over the proceedings seems to quell the nerves a bit. With that in mind, here is my list of things to take in with you, which covers Dad and bubs, too.

For you

Comfortable clothes. However long you plan to stay at the hospital, take clothes that you feel good in. You might be happy shuffling around in pjs and a dressing gown, or you might want to get dressed, so take several sets of whatever makes you feel most relaxed.

Slippers or **flipflops.** You will be walking the halls and in and out of the bathroom, so having something covering your feet is always wise.

Toiletries. Toothbrush, perfume, deodorant, make up (to feel nice after all that pushing), hairbrush, hair ties/hairband, pads, oils both for the room and for your body (I found wax melts worked great in the room and almond oil was lovely for massaging into my skin), Arnica cream or gel (helps with bruising), lip balm (gas and air can leave you with chapped lips) moisturiser, nipple cream and nipple pads, haemorrhoid cream (don't ask, just pack).

Swimsuit (tankini). Take this or a comfortable bra top if you're planning to use a birthing pool.

Going-home outfit. Pick out something nice. You did it, so now it's time to feel good and show off a bit. Don't forget that you might be feeding, so pack a bra and top that are suitable for nursing.

Bits and pieces. TENS machine, book, cards, puzzle books (it can be a long wait), a tablet or laptop to watch TV on, something to play music on, your mobile phone and all the accompanying plugs and chargers, candles (LED), birthing ball, sweet and savoury snacks (I've got chocolate buttons for a sugar pick-me-up and crisps for the salt, drinks, and finally, a camera or video camera (if you're not planning on using your phone for this).

Your birth choices. I've purposely called it choices because we are all aware that things never quite go to plan, so it's good to write down or record the things you want. This way, you, your birth partner and your midwife have something to refer back to. Here are some all-important questions that you need to consider. Do you want to be offered pain relief or to ask for it? How do you want to deliver, upright or lying down? (Personally, I'm going for upright, to let gravity help me.) Who is cutting the cord, and when? Are you wanting immediate skin-to-skin? (I advise yes, as it's so beneficial for both you and bubs.) Do you want to deliver the placenta naturally, or to be assisted? Breast or bottle? Do you want support in first-bath techniques?

For him

A **change of clothes** and some **swim trunks** for if you are using a birthing pool and he would either like to join you or support you closely from the side.

For your wee one

Several cute-as-a-button **outfits, nappies** and **wipes, bottom cream, flannels** for little spills, **muslins** for big spills and to wrap them in, **blankets**, a **car seat,** including a **headrest** (note, it's good to practise getting this in and out of the car before bubs arrives), **hats and/or mittens, bottles** and **formula** if you're not planning to breastfeed, and **toys** for the cot.

Pack this bag with your partner, as it will help for them to know where everything is when you need it, rather than you having to come out of the birthing bubble to get things yourself.

Remember to take some deep breaths and keep in mind that after everything, you will be a parent, so try and enjoy the process. It'll all be worth it. X

Daddy Time ... Bond style

Men can get sidelined when it comes to being a new parent. They get relegated to helper, the person who gives Mum a break rather than actually indulging in Daddy Time. This can take its toll on the father, and in the worst-case scenario prevent him from bonding with his child. He could lose interest or feel inadequate and overwhelmed, or even jealous. We need to make sure that dads get a look in and not be kept out of the parenting field. It took both of you to make this little person and it will take two of you to raise them! Fathers can get ignored in the chaos of having a new baby at home. Mothers get a rush of hormones, while fathers can only watch from the sidelines.

I've found you need to coax men into being present sometimes, and that can mean leaving them alone – alone with the wee one. Women have the added pressure that comes with the expectation they will know what they are doing. Like in *The Matrix*, it's thought we get an instant download to the brain and off we go. Dads, I suspect, miss out on that download and most of the time they are left with an error message. We need to remember that they are learning, too. They are not just your support crew; you need to give them bubs, walk out of the room and trust them to figure it out.

I have found that I have to let him do things. A bottle here and there (even though I'm breastfeeding) won't hurt, as getting them to make it up and give it to the baby can instill confidence. Also get them involved in bathtime. Admittedly, sometimes that ends up with my daughter being waterboarded with a flannel, but she survives, crucially after giving up where I have hidden the clothes, chocolates and other spontaneous purchases made when I thought she was asleep – the little traitor! I also have to sit on my hands as he changes her, lifting her by her ankles clean off the mat. When I hear her giggling away, I know he's doing OK. But don't get me started on allowing him to dress her . . . all those spontaneous purchases of matching little socks and dresses go out of the window and she ends up in a mismatched top and pants in a kaleidoscope of colours that make her look like she's just got back from Woodstock or joined a hippy commune. But he looks so proud of himself that he got her into something in the first place, and we have likened the process to getting an octopus into a string bag. The expletives about buttons, poppers and tights would send this sentence blue. Trust me when I say that Bub's first word won't be Mama or Dada! I often have to bite my lip not to point out that whatever he's dressed her in is also on back to front . . .

My favourite times are when we are having a New Parent Date Night – with a takeaway and the latest blockbuster downloaded – and she will either be playing or asleep on his chest, or when we are out in all weathers, with wellies and coats if needed, and she's strapped to his chest, with him protecting her from the elements. So, Bond up (Google Daniel Craig with baby sling) and give bubs to him. If they are strapped to Dad, you can even hold hands. It's been scientifically and genetically proven that in their first year of life, babies look like their fathers. This is so the dads will claim them – obviously the mother already knows that it's her baby! This harks back to caveman days, when people didn't necessarily know a child's paternity (saucy!) yet mothers needed a father to hunt and gather for them. It's still in men's DNA to want to provide for their offspring. Thank goodness we can teach our little ones better gender roles, but, saying that, if you have a man around then let him give into his urges (of parenting, that is!).

Remember, he is not just there to give you a break, he is there, hopefully, as a fully functioning parent and member of the family. As time goes by, it's helpful for both father and child to actually pencil in time with each other. Perhaps by taking a bike ride together, with the wee one strapped to his bike and the wind in their faces, laughing in pure enjoyment. Or by going on secret adventures or even just to walk to buy the paper or something. When I was a nanny, I had one dad who, when they were in season, would take his daughter and then subsequent children on a walk every Saturday to buy a pineapple. Then they would bring it home, peel it and devour it – just them! Those kids are now in their twenties and remember those days every time they see a pineapple. People say it's either the quality or the quantity of time you spend with your child. In my twenty-five years of watching parents with their kids and adding to that my experience of being a new mum, I can wholeheartedly say it should be both every time.

There are a lot of good dads out there and we need to make sure we acknowledge them and give them time to shine. Now, I'll have to stop writing and go and show my other half how to put a new front pack on . . . he has her legs akimbo.

Baby Babble Babel Fish

Trust thy baby, which really means trust thyself, as right now, they are an extension of you. It's not just that they came of you and from you, but at this moment in time, they are you. Essentially, they need you completely to keep them alive, just as you would yourself. They are wholly helpless and reliant on you. Just as you would feed yourself, keep yourself warm and sleep when you need to, they need you to do the same for them. The two (or three or more, depending on your support circle) of you need to work in harmony to achieve this. And that's where the tricky bit comes in: *communication*. Because they are a separate person but need what you need, you have to learn each other's language. And for some new parents, and heck, second and third-time parents, this can be scary. They are crying, like all the time, and you don't know what they want or need. Don't panic, as here is a secret – you do know what they want and need, you just have to trust yourself. And listen: one to yourself and two to them, as they are telling you everything you need to know.

Firstly, it's vital to listen to yourself, as in the first few weeks and months you are in charge. If you think they are hungry, they probably are, so feed them. If you feel cold, pop an extra layer on them, too. Just one, though. They only need one extra layer and won't appreciate being bundled up like a Christmas ham! If your inner mummy voice is saying they are tired, then put them to sleep. In a way, that works for both of you. For example, if they like to be swaddled and rocked, or need the boob to help them settle, then that's what you do. Sleep 'training' and putting them down to sleep rather than asleep comes later. Check their nappy is clean, not bunched up (no one likes a wedgie, no matter what age) or too tight and pinching, etc. If they are fussing, check that a hand, or in the case of my bubs her ear, isn't bent in a funny way and annoying them as they lie in your arms.

Secondly, listen to them, as they are telling you what they need. Their cry is their communication, and when you have mastered how to decipher it, it's as clear as speaking. It's their own little language and you can and will learn it. Also, it is unique to them, just as their little voices will be in the years to come. Think back to when you last travelled to a foreign country and had to learn a bit of the lingo – it's like that. You will pick it up and you will pick it up quickly, trust me. Although in full disclosure, I have 'travelled' a lot, as I was a nanny for over twenty years and learned the lingo of many babies. There are definite similarities, so I had a head start when it came to my own bubs.

Babies have a wet/uncomfortable cry, a hungry cry, a tired cry, and an annoyed cry. And you will intrinsically know them, as they will reflect in your own emotions. When I say that, I don't mean what you are feeling at that time, although the annoyed, nothing-is-right cry might be shared at 2am! No, what I mean should become clear from the following examples:

> » The tired cry is a long, drawn out cry that you will recognise when you are tired – it's almost a grizzle.

> » The hungry cry is a short and sharp cry that says, "I'm starving and need food now." Most of us have experienced that feeling.

> » The wet cry is one where they squirm, too, indicating they are physically uncomfortable.

> » The annoyed cry is like it says on the tin – they sound peeved. That's the hardest one to combat, as nothing is right and you just have to calm them down the best way you can after trying everything else: food, cuddle and a clean bum.

You will soon become a dab hand at all of this and even be able to predict the mood and needs of your baby before they hit the decibels. This will be a blessing to everyone, including your neighbours and/or strangers in the street. So, put your Babel Fish in your ear (for those that haven't read the book or seen the TV show, this is a reference from *The Hitchhiker's Guide to the Galaxy*) and start listening to and hearing your child. You will soon relax, and they will too, knowing that both of you are in good hands.

The Off Switch

You have survived the first couple of weeks, when experienced people were on hand to offer you their support and advice. Your wee one slept and ate and pooped, before repeating everything in no particular order, and you were happy just to go with the flow. Now it's week six, it's 2 am and your bundle of joy is awake, wide awake. They have been fed, burped and changed, and they are warm and should be in the land of nod. Only they can't quite get there, and they are looking to you to help them. I am of the school of thought that says parenting is a two-way street, between you and your child. You make suggestions, which they then either accept or refuse, and then it's up to you to reinforce the mutual decision (more on this later). So, when they are asking you to help them fall asleep, I have some tried and tested methods of identifying the best ways to do this. I call this their 'off switch', and like a dial on a safe, the combination is unique to every little one.

All babies have a way they like to be calmed and soothed, so they can relax into sleep, and it's up to you to find that sweet spot. They want and need you to press it for them. I have found that it is usually a combination of the techniques that follow and/or physical touch. So, I will get right to the point of how to find it. Every child's switch is different, so what works for one won't work for the other. But here are the keys to finding their combination. These techniques are for very wee ones. Once you have a routine and you are putting them down to sleep rather than getting them asleep, you won't need these anymore.

The snuggle pose. Cradle your child, facing you, with their bottom in your palm, their head in the crook of your arm and their legs tucked around your body. This will give them an all-encompassing feeling of comfort. They can smell you, see you, hear your breathing and your heartbeat, and feel you all the way around them. You can add touch to that, as you can use your other hand to stroke them. There are a few places that have a calming effect. These include stroking their hairline from their forehead to ear, and then back again. But the best technique when you need them to sleep is to stroke their nose (not to the tip, as it's so sensitive that it will wake them up again). I call this the off button. You can also stroke down over their eyes ever so gently with your fingertips. Do all this while gently humming or singing; the vibrations of your voice alone can help settle your child.

Close to your heart. Holding your baby on your chest, while you're either standing, sitting or lying down, is a wonderful position for both of you. Have them positioned over your heart with their head just under your chin and your arms holding them around their bottom. Not much can get done in this position except sleeping or dozing for both of you, but it's a wonderful way to bond, as baby listens to your breathing and heartbeat. I've heard this position called the 'daddy mattress', as it's usually dads who find it comfortable.

Over the shoulder holder. Placing your child in the crook of your arm, or with their bottom in your palm, rest their head either over your shoulder or snuggled into your neck. Your other arm should be on their back, gently holding them. They will appreciate the warmth and scent of your neck, and this position allows for easy jiggling and back patting. You can free up one arm if needed. It also allows you to move around and pace the house to help them settle. For some reason, known only to your child, they like to be upright and sometimes over your shoulder to fall asleep. This position frees up their airways and they can snuggle into you for comfort. It's a winner for both parent and child.

Once you have your comfortable position sorted, be it on your shoulder, in your arms or on your chest, you will need to find out which jiggle works for your baby. I have defined them here, and you'll find that there will be one, or a combination of a few jiggles, that will be exactly what your child needs to sleep. As soon as you find the winning combination, you will hold the key to helping your child find a peaceful transition into sleep. Be warned, though, you may not find their jiggle straight away. It can be littered with trial and error, squeaky floorboards and a few false starts.

The swing. Plant your feet apart so that you're comfortable, as you'll need a stable base. From the hips, swing from side to side, quickly to begin with, before slowing down as your baby settles. If they are calm initially, the motion will quickly send them off to sleep. If they're unsettled, it will have a meditative effect, giving them nothing to concentrate on.

The bouncy. For this, you need to get into the same position as you did for the swing, keeping your feet planted firmly apart, with your child in a comfortable position. Bouncing from either arm can get tiring, so try doing this from your knees. As with the swing, it's the feeling of a rhythmic movement that helps bubs to settle and/ or calm down if they are loudly voicing their opinion. I suspect the element of movement and distraction is what makes it work so well.

The half jiggle. Again, get into a comfortable position and then jiggle with the arm that is closest to bubs, while holding them. Do short, sharp movements from the elbow, which only jiggle the baby's lower half. This one is a great workout for the arms, and I find it useful as a quick and easy short soother if bubs doesn't require much to settle.

The bum pat. I find that a lot of people do this naturally with bubs, and it's performed at all times of the day and in every place, seated or walking around, to settle or offer reassurance. It involves holding your baby across the middle with one arm, with them facing inwards to you. Use your other arm to pat their bottom while cradling it. Note, I have not said gently here, as I have found that babies quite like a good pat. I am in NO way advocating smacking or hitting your child, but they're wearing some very padded protection, so you don't need to be too soft.

The bum pat can also be used when they are lying in their beds. This is easy when they are older and on their sides or tummy (once they can roll, they will choose to sleep on their stomachs!), but when they are little you can raise their legs up and to the side a little and pat their bottoms gently, just to finally settle them. I have found that this jiggle also works for night reassurances, which you can do without getting them up or out of bed. A little bum jiggle in the dark can help them resettle, allowing you to go straight back to bed.

I've found that I naturally combine a number of these jiggles, and a well-worn pacing pattern around the room will help you to find your baby's key to sleep. For instance, you might find that a bum pat with a swing or a half jiggle and a bounce works well. When trying to find your baby's preferred jiggle routine, give each one about five minutes. If your child is still protesting after this time, move on to the next method. I promise that you will see an instant signal from your baby when you find the right jiggle or combination of jiggles. Remember to also remain calm yourself. Go to your happy place, no matter what the noise level becomes. Your baby can read your body language better then you can read theirs, it's all they've got to go on! Take deep breaths while gently humming, singing or whispering soothing words. This will all help your child to quickly find their quiet place.

There will be those times when your child is lost to their emotions. They will not know what they want and even if they did, they wouldn't be able to tell you. They may be ill, over stimulated, overtired, or plain frustrated. Covering all the basics: food, warmth, clean bottom, trapped wind, etc., hasn't worked and they just need help to calm down. But, as you'll know, when legs are flailing and arms are everywhere (and that's just you!) and bubs is arching their back and thrashing their head around, the jiggles I've explained won't work, as they're for a nice quiet baby, which right now you haven't got!

I have found that due to the lack of verbal communication available, in these situations you need to stick to what you know. Having worked out their combination from above you need to push through the emotion. Your baby now needs you to show them the way to calm. Go through your steps: music, darkened room, etc. 'But what about the thrashing and flailing?' I hear you ask. Yes, I know it's like watching an invading army, in this case an emotional baby, but simply stand your ground. Hold them in the positions they favour, holding them right up against you at first before moving them into a cradling position once they've begun to calm down. Hold them as best you can, letting their arms flail out and their legs fly free. I find that instead of holding their legs to you, it's best to hold a hand in between them, so they can kick out if they want to. Let them get it out of their system, but in a place of safety (your arms) and comfort.

The boa constrictor. A baby that wants to settle but can't find the way doesn't want to be pinned to you, so place your body and arms in a way so that they are held but not confined. Then, as you persevere with your settling routine and they begin to calm, you can pull them in closer. Judge their body language, and if they look to be settling, tuck their legs into you. This may involve a few false starts as they kick out again, but simply let them reset and then start again. Now, slowly and gently tuck the arm that is half flailing back to you. Think of this action as kind of like mimicking a boa constrictor. After catching its prey, this large snake tightens its grip around it with every breath. I am by NO means advocating strangling your child, but as they settle, draw them closer to you so they can feel and regulate their breathing with yours. They will be able to recognise your scent and hear your heartbeat, which was the very first comforting sound they ever heard. This should lull them into peace and maybe sleep, if that's what is needed. I find that this can also work just to calm them and bring them back to a happy state, where they can then go on to play or eat, etc.

Listen for The Hump

Every baby has a breath that signifies when they have decided to settle, which I call The Hump. It sounds like a double breath when they are upset, or a long breath when they are sleepy. Sometimes it's a drawn-out grizzle instead, one that sounds almost half-hearted. I call it The Hump because it's like reaching the top of a hill – you'll know it'll be easier on the way down and the main work is over. In your case, you're on the way towards having a happy or sleepy baby.

You are now armed (pun intended) with all the physical knowledge you need to read your baby's code and work out what will help them to settle. Just remember that these techniques are really only for times of great need, as you will eventually move towards putting your baby down to sleep rather than getting them to sleep. This is when looking out for signs that they are ready for some shut eye can be invaluable. I have found that there is a window about fifteen minutes before they go to sleep. They will yawn, pull an ear, wriggle, stretch or blink slowly, and this is your cue to pop them into bed or a sleeping area (a car seat or pram, etc.) They will then snuggle down and drift off of their own accord, with no 'switching off' required. This is the holy grail and will come with time, practice and observation on both sides. This also harks back to the two-way street I spoke about in the first paragraph of this blog, which I employ with my child. She makes a suggestion, such as "I'm tired", and I reinforce this by putting her somewhere to sleep. In this way, we are communicating and forming a routine regarding our expectations of each other.

Your baby's sleeping patterns and preferred ways of doing things don't have to be a minefield, or a scary affair that leaves all parties exhausted and just doing whatever works each night. Finding the combination to unlock your baby's off switch will ensure both you and your child find a peaceful and settled solution to getting them to sleep faster, and without the stress that can be felt in the first few months of new parenthood. Just like you have your own combination that helps you to relax, be that a warm bath, reading for a few minutes and/or drinking some chamomile tea, so does your baby. You and your child speak to each other in a variety of ways, and learning each other's wants and needs is just another part of falling in love with this perfect little person. Sweet dreams.

Dream Feeder

I believe you can get me through the night . . .

Sorry, I have that song lyric stuck in my head. It's from *Dream Weaver* by Gary Wright, and it also featured in the movie *Wayne's World* (I'm showing my age a bit here). When I sat down to start writing this post, the song would not stop playing on repeat in my head. And it does fit nicely into this blog, as dream feeding has got me through many a night, and my wee woman's nights too. I am not saying this to show off, I just know that a) mums need to know that dream feeding does exist and can give them a whole night's sleep, and b) your baby can do it too. I have been practising dream feeding and helping mums with it for more than twenty-five years, and it's what has worked for me and them. I am sharing the information here, as it might just work for you too.

Here's what I do. For the first couple of weeks, I do whatever the/my baby wants, while writing down sleep and feeding times. Slowly, a pattern will emerge. The point is that this routine is fluid, and if you relax and just see what your baby is doing, nights will become less stressful. Being a new mum is hard because you're supposed to know what you're doing, and you may feel pressure to be doing this, that or the other. There is always some kid that is sleeping through the night when yours isn't, and that puts added pressure on you. You may get to the point when you're so tired you can't see straight, and you are sick of everyone telling you what to do. We've all been there.

Anyway, I'll now get to the point and tell you how I mastered dream feeding, because if you're sleep deprived, you just need to hear it straight. So, I take note of patterns and see what works for her, so I can then 'suggest' this pattern to her. For example, my baby catnaps throughout the day. This works for me, as I have step-children and there isn't a set nap time (she's three months old and has to fit into her family commitments), but she has consistently slept in the evening between around 7 and 9 pm, either in my arms, the bassinet (when she was younger) or on the couch (when she was a little older). She will wake for a quick breastfeed and kick about time then have a bottle between 9.30 and 10.30 pm (she will tell me when she's ready for it), before settling down for the night at 11 pm. I go to bed sometime after this, and that's when I dream feed her. For some reason, my breasts haven't joined in on the scheduling and so I don't really have enough milk in the evening (I've tried pumping to get the supply up, but we were both getting frustrated, hence the bottle), but they fill up like balloons at 11.30 pm onwards. So, we have a darkened room, her music playing, Ewan the sheep to hand and she's in her bed sleep bag thing and I'm in my comfy pjs. We're in my bed and I feed her sideways. This way, when she's asleep she can just latch on from the smell. I feed her from both sides, burp her and then give her an extra-long cuddle, as I know these times go so fast and she has a super soft head that is sleepy and tucked into my neck. Then I put her into her cot, which, at present, is next to my bed. When she goes into her own room, this routine will be conducted from a rocking chair.

For bubs, this little top up seems to see her through the night. She usually stirs around 6 am, and although she doesn't quite wake, she tells me she's ready for another feed. We repeat the cycle, and then she sleeps on until our day fully begins. The thinking and science behind the dream feed is to *top them up* without *waking them up*. I don't wait until she is fully awake and then needs to be resettled, rather my plan is to give her that bit more last thing at night, in the hope that this will link in with her sleep cycles. As a nanny, I suggested this to mums and then, when their children were older, I advised to let them sip on a bottle of water whenever they woke in the night. They soon realised that this was not worth waking up for and slept through. The dream feed can be from a bottle or a breast. And it's done for both you and your baby's convenience. It can be easily written into the night-time routine of, say, bath, new nappy bed and bottle (or breast). When they do wake in the night, take note of whether it is for comfort or food. If you upped the bottle or dream feed, would it get them over that hump and help them go longer? If you are having to get them up, make sure you don't fully wake them and change their nappy in dimmed light. And feed them in the dark, too – you will both go back to sleep faster.

Now, I know that this is trial and error, and that this system may not work for you and your family, and that's OK, but I hope that this or something else does. We mums have so much on our plates that a lack of sleep can seem inevitable, though I don't think it has to be. With a bit of observation, both you and your baby can find your rhythm and work together to get through the night.

Minding their Ps and Qs (patterns and cues) - My 'Ish' Plan

My baby is getting bigger; she is four months old now and is becoming more and more bossy. The other day, she even had her first tantrum. Her dad and I weren't helping, as we were smiling and saying, "Ooh, look, her first tanty, isn't she cute!" But she was trying to tell us something and we obviously weren't listening. What she was attempting to say, and finally did tell me, was that she was tired and wanted to be put to bed. I know this because once I stopped goggling at her, I saw her cues and got her settled with her muslin and dummy, and then she went straight to sleep. Her cue is a wee meow sort of noise. She does this about fifteen minutes before she wants to rest and she'll also rub her eyes and then keep playing, smiling or feeding, etc., which means the cue may be missed, especially as she only does it a few times and expects me to pick up on it. For first-time mums, this kind of behaviour can be daunting.

With this type of cue, your baby is telling you that they agree with what you have suggested for them and need you to go through with it. You see, over the months, they will have clocked onto you wanting them to sleep, eat, play, not poop (though no one has control over that one!). They are learning the difference between day and night, awake and asleep times and playtimes, etc. And over the months, loose patterns will emerge that work for you both. Babies like routine. This has to be very movable, as life changes daily, be that within the family or through things coming up, such as doctors' visits, classes, clinics and coffee dates. So, to fit in with their loose pattern, you might need to let them have a quick catnap in the car or feed them at a friend's house or on a park bench. I refer to this fluidity as the 'ish' of life, and it's good for you both. Babies like to know what's happening next, and as a mum you need to be fluid with that while staying within the realms of both your expectations.

So, as life calms down and starts to take shape, take note of when your baby likes to sleep, as it will usually be around the same times every day. Mine likes to go back down around two hours after she has woken. These 'ish' times will slowly form a schedule that you can make plans around. As for feeding, I tend to feed on demand, so I only take note of evening feeds. I give her a bottle before bed (she's got herself into a wee routine of breastfeed, catnap, playtime, bottle, burp and bed, then a dream feed at 11ish). Once they get bigger and move onto solids, there will be more set times, i.e., snack and mealtimes, that you can evolve into a schedule. But that's exactly the point, your baby, like mine, will alert you to their needs and then you can act on them. My daughter suggests something to me (more like demands it loudly), and I reinforce it – it's a mutual agreement that works for us both.

If you look at these patterns – the ones they have come up with and the ones you have introduced – you can then work together to achieve a rhythm in your family life. There is nothing more stressful to a new mum, or any parent, than when you have someone or something, i.e., a book, saying they should be sleeping for exactly two hours, drinking this much milk, pooping that much and staying awake for this long, etc. It's stressful for a parent who doesn't know what their baby wants or needs to feel pressured into doing things a certain way, which may not work. For instance, at the set sleep times you might find them wailing throughout! I had a mum call me in tears, as her book said her baby daughter should be asleep between 9 and 11 am, but she wasn't dropping off until 9.45, meaning she was still tired when woken. I advised the mum to throw away her book and read her child instead. The fact she wasn't falling asleep until 9.45 meant this was the ideal time to put her down and then allow her to sleep for however long she needed to. Some kids do morning sleeps, some afternoon ones. While that may mean changing your plans to fit around their ideal snooze times, remember, a happy baby equals a happy mummy.

So, back to my bossy boots of a daughter. Who are we kidding that she's not the one in charge at the moment? There's no reasoning with her, so I have no choice but to listen to her and implement her needs into my day, so that we can both be happy. I have to try and read her patterns while accepting that they can and will change in an instant, like a kaleidoscope. But I am there for her, and I do indicate what she should be doing next, as although she may be in charge, she has no idea what she is doing. But boy, try telling her that . . . I can see this being another pattern in our lives.

Shhh, the nine S's

Said gently to a distressed baby, shhh can bring peace, comfort and quiet. We say it automatically, as our parents and grandparents said it before us. Hopefully, our children will go on to calm their babies with it, too. The American paediatrician Harvey Karp famously came up with five 'S' words that calm a child, but in my experience, I say there are nine. These all lead into each other and all are vital to helping your child to calm and then to self-settle.

Shhh. This can be our first response to a distressed baby. Usually, it's said gently to soothe them, but try saying it louder, right in their ear. From inside the womb onwards, babies are used to noise. Filling their world with sound (white noise) will distract them from whatever is bothering them.

Smell. When you are close, they will be able to detect your scent. And it's a familiar comfort. If you want to get Dad involved in soothing or getting bubs to sleep, wear one of his t-shirts for a couple of nights. Let it absorb all your scents; breast milk, perfume, soaps and lotions, etc., and then give it back to him to wear when he's around the little one. If it's an emergency, pop a used breast pad between his chest and bubs, and this will work as an instant pacifier.

Safe. Babies like to feel safe and secure. When they feel your body heat and listen to your heartbeat, it reminds them of being in the womb. If they are flailing their arms and legs while thrashing their heads as they try to find a comfortable spot, pull them in a wee bit tighter, to remind them that you are there.

Swaddle. You will know how your baby likes to be wrapped, and if you don't, they will tell you! Tight or loose, arms in or arms out, it takes trial and error to get the folds just right for your baby, but do keep at it. Sometimes, it is exactly what they need in order to settle. There is a school of thought now that discourages swaddling, as it's believed that if it's done too tightly it will risk baby's hips misaligning or causing them to overheat, especially if using modern, synthetic fabrics. I have swaddled babies throughout my career and have continued this method as a parent. I use a super large muslin to wrap bubs in. This is surprisingly warm, breathable and soft, and it takes on the family smell. You can buy specially designed and shaped natural fibre blankets and materials for swaddling. They even come with directions!

Swing. Movement is distracting and familiar to bubs. They were sloshed and swished around inside Mum for nine months. So, get moving. Dance, bounce, sway and swing – whatever you want to do. The act of movement will distract them, as they won't be able to focus on anything else. The combination of white noise in the form of you gently shushing them and the sway/swing action will lull them into a state of calm. As they settle, and before your arms drop off, you can also slow down. I also find a bum pat is a good one to add to the mix, as if needed, it can be continued after you have put them down.

Sideways. We have all been held like this, and generations of babies will be after us, too. Their heads are on your chest, with the length of their body along your arm. You can then tuck in the arm closest to you, so they are snug into your body and can listen to your heartbeat and breathing.

Stroke. Gently stroking around your baby's forehead, eyebrows and down between their eyes (what people call the T-zone) will help them to let go of the visual world and drift off. Remember, they are learning, computing and taking in everything they see and hear, so it's hard for them to switch off – you have to help them. I find that this can also be done once you have put them down. It will reassure them that you are still there before they completely surrender to the land of nod.

Suck. It's up to you whether it's a bottle, nipple, dummy/pacifier/binky, their thumb or yours, but sucking has a wonderful calming effect on bubs when they are upset. It's a natural reflex from inside the womb, when they would practise swallowing and sucking before falling asleep or having some quiet time. The act is physically distracting, so it takes them away from what is mentally or physically bothering them. For instance, they might have been hungry or peckish, or just in need of some comfort.

Snuggle. We all love a good snuggle, especially with a warm and lovely baby, and the good news is that they like this, too. Sometimes, the act of either holding them and talking to them face to face or allowing them to watch the world go by from the safety of your arms is all they want. When there is danger, the safest place for a baby is in their parent's arms. Don't underestimate the power of just snuggling, either in bed in the morning or at night, or on the couch. They instinctively know this to be a good place, and holding them will reaffirm this.

So, as you can see, the nine S's – Shhh, Smell, Safety/Security, Swaddle, Sway/Swing, Sideways, Stroke, Suck and Snuggle are all Super important to the wellbeing of you and your baby. They can be combined or used on their own. You will soon discover the unique combination that will help your baby to settle. Eventually, they will use some of the techniques themselves, in order to self-settle. My bubs needs her dummy and a muslin next to her face while holding her own hand for comfort. She is doing the Smell (muslin), Suck (dummy) and the Safe (holding her hand). I provide the Snuggle and the Stroke and, if needed, the Shhh. Although, when she gets herself into a real state, I use ALL of the S's to help her find her happy place. And you can, too.

Roll With It

As a nanny, my kids never grew up as such, as once they started school, they didn't need me anymore and I would go on to work with another baby. This means I have moved a lot of wee ones in my time while not wanting to disturb them. This blog is about sleeping babies and how to transfer them around the place, from arms to cot, from person to person and from car seat to cot/pushchair. I'm old school and I like the old ways of doing things, such a swaddling, as I know they work. When I finally had my own baby, I had a discussion with my health visitor about how the school of thought had moved on from swaddling. Regardless, I swaddled my child and I also 'rolled' her, as in popped a rolled-up blanket behind and in front of her, which helped to get her to sleep and then to keep her asleep on her side, in what's known as the rescue position, which you also do during first aid. If you look up 'roll sleeping baby' online, you will find many devices and specialised baby beds that will help you to successfully achieve this technique. I found it worked for me, as my wee one slept through the night this way from the age of six weeks. As she has grown, I have continued with the roll technique. I no longer roll her between blankets, but I continue to carry her and pick her up in a certain way as if she was. What I mean by this is that when they are swaddled, you have to support them through their head, shoulders and, finally, both parts of their torso, from their shoulders to their bum. I continue to lift her this way, as it's familiar and, therefore, comfortable for her, and I find she remains asleep throughout.

I have tried and tested different ways of moving a sleeping baby. Here is how I did/do it.

Flat hands. Think of your baby like a pancake. When they are sleeping and you want to move them, you need to ensure you bear their weight evenly. I have found that if you grab them, especially under their arms, it instantly wakes them up. If they are asleep on you, they are usually lying flat on your chest or in the crook of your arm. When you need to move, or move them, keep a flat platform, holding them close to you. This works right from when they are a baby to toddlerhood. When they are asleep (and you want to keep it that way), your child needs to feel safe and contained. Touching their skin or raising their body parts up will jolt them out of the REM (rapid eye movement) stage of sleep, and they will take a while to settle again. Covering as much of their body as you can with warm hands will help them to feel secure. So, place your palms flat against them, keeping the pressure through your hands and fingers even. Poking and prodding them will only wake them.

Python hold. Whenever I employ this technique, I use both hands and approach my wee one from both sides. To help them feel secure with flat hands, I try to encompass their whole body, sliding one arm under their shoulder blades and bringing the other around their bum. I have found this especially useful when doing the transfer from car seat to cot. I take the straps off them, ensuring that I move their limbs using their clothing. This is because touching their skin awakens their senses (literally) and rouses them, so the less contact the better. I slide one arm under their top half and the other under their bottom half, so that when I raise them up, they curl into my body. You can also put your bottom hand through their legs and lift them out of the car seat that way, scooping them towards you. Another variation is to lift them by the scruff of their clothes, which acts as a sling, holding the baby's weight. Babygrows are particularly good for this. However, this is only for when they are little and light enough. When they are older, you can still use their clothes to raise them up enough so you can get your arm underneath them. Just make sure you have a good hold in order to balance out the weight distribution.

Roll them towards or away from you. Whenever you are moving them, be it from you to the couch so you can go pee, to another's arms or out of the pushchair or car seat, try to roll them along your arms. In their sleep, children naturally turn over onto their sides or go all the way over onto their tummies, so the sensation of rolling will not fully wake them up. I found that I could transfer my wee one to her Daddy's arm when we joined them together to make one arm. We would put our crooked arms next to each other and then roll her over the gap and into Dad's waiting crook. If you drop them, the feeling of falling, even the smallest bit, arouses their senses. If she is sleeping like this, I roll my wee one out of the car seat. I python hold her then roll her gently towards my body, nestling her face in my neck. That aspect is important on two counts. One, you smell right. Your baby has been asleep in your neck from day dot. It's their happy place. Your perfume, deodorant and body smell is strongest in the crook of your neck. So, when they're being lifted, your scent provides instant security to a sleepy brain. Two, it's dark. No matter what you do, your baby will stir, but by rolling them into a dark, safe place, they will soon relax again.

Wave technique/headfirst. When a baby has been in your arms and you want to put them down, it's very important to do it right, or else your hard work getting them settled may be undone in an instant. The trick when putting them into either a cot or a pushchair is to place them down headfirst, as in head down, as if you are making a wave shape. Tilt their body and yours towards the mattress at an angle. It sounds strange but trust me, it works. Place their head down first then allow their body to lower itself vertebrae by vertebrae. Think pilates, yoga or even weights, as these are all exercises where you lower yourself down slowly. Let the action flow like a wave shape, ending it gently by putting down their feet. I have found that if you place them flat, it can rouse them. Also, the extra movement of sliding your hands out from underneath them alerts them to a disruption in their equilibrium. With your flat hands, let them pour (they are all floppy anyway) out of your arms, and then you can release your hold without them really noticing.

Pyramid scheme. I have found that when they are already lying down asleep, it can be hard to get them up and into your arms, especially if you haven't had hold of them already (as in, they've been asleep in the crook of your now dead arm). So, picking them up can be tricky. But if you scoop them up from each side of their waist with flat palms, you can sort of sweep your hands under and up, taking their weight on your forearms, so (fingers crossed) they don't notice they are being elevated. It's a bit like lifting them from water. You bring your hands together at their heads, raising them up towards you and either nestling them into your neck or, if you can keep them flat-ish like a pizza, transferring them silently into their cot, using the reverse method to lay them flat. This explains the nickname pyramid, as to begin with, you are making a triangle with your arms. This method is also good for stiff or tired backs, as you take the weight in your shoulders, forearms and wrists.

I try to have the bed ready, with a muslin or wrap already in place on the mattress, so once they're down they can be bundled up tight, if that's how they feel secure. Alternatively, I'll have a blanket on hand to tuck them in. The curtains will already be closed, making the transaction as seamless as possible. Sometimes, this means leaving them to sleep in the car for a few minutes while I whip inside to prepare, or I leave the car running and the radio on while I get the pushchair sorted.

It's also important to get the timing right. There's no point transferring a sleeping child who is either just coming out of a sleep cycle or is too far in one. I have found that children's sleep cycles are around forty-five minutes, and once they learn to link sleep cycles, they usually nap during the daytime for around ninety minutes or so. If you need to transfer them, you need to do it within fifteen minutes of them falling asleep, or it can be too disruptive, and they will wake and then not settle back down again. Think of how you are when you get woken up from a deep sleep. If you have missed the window, park up, catch up with a friend on the phone or take a nap yourself. A sleep every so often in the car seat won't do them any harm, but to aid the development of their back, don't make this an everyday habit.

I know every child is different and unique in how they like or dislike things to happen to them. So, if none of this works for you then disregard it. It's simply a suggestion based on what I have found to work for the children I have helped to raise. But if it works for you in the slightest and thus earns you a bit of extra down time, then I'm glad I was able to share it.

Strip and Dip

One of the most wonderful times with your baby is when they are naked! Firstly, the skin-on-skin contact you had when they were born and whenever you could get it in the first weeks, and now during bathtime or shower time. This is a wonderful bonding moment that you can carve out for you and your baby. It can last a few minutes to half an hour, or more if you include baby massage, and it can be whenever you want it to be. If you're a busy mum then take them into the shower with you – I do. I have everything ready – her towel and a wash cloth – and I bring her into the bathroom, let the room get all warm and steamy and then I undress her, leaving her lying on a nappy and able to have a kick with her knickers off, so to speak. Then I jump in, do my thing and grab her for the last few minutes. She loves the water on her back and head and instantly relaxes into my arms, where we can just meld together. She's taken to licking her lips as the water comes over her face. It's a great way to get babies reintroduced to water and leads onto swim time later. Babies naturally like water, providing you reintroduce it to them early on and they don't get waterboarded (like my partner does with her). What is it with dads and their functionality when it comes to having a wash? We mums understand the caress of water and the relaxation. Bubs does too, and if you're happy and relaxed then so are they.

That's why bathing time is an intricate part of a good routine. Not only does it get them clean – as we all know, by the end of the day everyone is covered in spills and sick ups – it gives you both time to relax. The routine of bathtime is so important later in the winding down for a full night's sleep. For older kids, it transforms into bath, book, bed. It is an early signifier that the day is coming to an end. So, starting this routine early is great. A warm fluffy towel, a smiling face on the side of the bath or in it with them, and water surrounding them, allowing them to float. Lovely smelly lotions and potions to wash them with and massage into their clean skin. As he towel dries our little one, my partner calls this 'the polish'. Massaging them helps them to release the day, allowing their limbs to stretch out and their lymph nodes to drain. It also helps the cognitive and physical patterns they've been learning to sink in, through synapses in the brain that are triggered with touch (the ear lobes and crossing their centre line with your feet and fingers). It's a wonderful time to connect with your baby through eye contact and singing or speaking to them. If you can't think of what to say, tell them about your day or what body part you are drying. You could also count their toes and fingers with them. It's during this type of one-on-one that they learn conversation and speech patterns. In later years, they will master how to count and name their body parts. Everything can be a learning experience!

So, please pop strip and dip into your routine – there really is nothing like sploshing warm water (they will start to relax as soon as they hear the bath running), stripping off the day's clothes and letting the air hit their skin, before submerging them into soapy suds, scooping them up in a towel and wrapping them up like a sausage roll. Then you can dry them off, smother them in kisses and raspberries on their bare tummy, dress them in soft pjs and have a sleepy, soapy smelling bubs in your arms ready for bed. Enjoy.

Tips and Tricks

I may know my stuff when it comes to looking after babies, after all, I am a qualified and experienced nanny, but I'm the first to admit that when it comes to motherhood, there is still so much to learn. So, I thought I would pass on some of the tips and tricks I have picked up over the past few weeks, which other first-time mums may find useful.

Breast pads. These aren't only great for leaks (which can happen when your baby cries, or you move funny and your top rubs against your nipple and then, hey presto, they both go off at the same time, like an errant water sprinkler), they can also be put to good use if you have Dad or someone helping out with a bottle feed or getting them to settle. Ask them to pop your breast pad between them and the baby, which will make them smell right, i.e., just like you.

Hot flannels. After you've fed your baby, your nipples will still be stimulated, which makes it hard, literally, for them to relax. So, have a warm flannel/facecloth ready to pop on your breast after it's been drained; it's like a mini massage and will start soothing you immediately. I also got some of those reusable gel hand warmers, which work wonders in the middle of the night. On the flipside, cucumber slices help to cool them down.

Onesies. The shoulder folds at the top are designed so that if an explosive poo occurs and it's all up their back and almost in their hair, you can get the garment off them from the shoulders down instead of up, which would only make the mess worse. This is a clever bit of design and seems obvious when you're in the know, but I was completely in the dark until a friend pointed it out and I had a light-bulb moment. Just remember, it's down not up.

Reflux in pregnancy. There are many over-the-counter and old wives' tale remedies to help with heartburn and reflux, and you may find that you are walking around mainlining Gaviscon with a straw in the bottle, but a fellow mum put me onto Love Hearts sweets or anything containing sherbet. It's pretty much the same and tastes a bit better. I found sucking on those much more enjoyable.

Reflux in babies. I have found that bubs sleeps better if I prop her up in bed using a small pillow or folded towel under her mattress. The slight tilt allows fluids to stay down and airways to remain clear. It is really helpful to keep any colic or reflux at bay. It's also really useful to do when babies have a cold, as they will get bunged up and have phlegm on their chests. The position will keep their airways clear and help them to sleep and get better. They may sound like Mr Snuffleupagus from *Sesame Street*, but they will sleep. You can, of course, buy special wedges for the propping, but I've found a simple pillow under the mattress works just as well.

Cradle cap. Rather than buying expensive shampoos that are full of chemicals, the trick is to use oil. And you can use any oil, be that olive, vegetable or coconut. Cradle cap is a harmless skin condition that will cause bub's scalp to go scaly and dry. This can become itchy and sore for them – it's basically dandruff, but a bit worse. So, when it starts (as it will, because they mostly have less hair to begin with, so their wee scalps are exposed to the elements), simply oil them up. I warm up a small container of oil in the microwave, so it's easy to apply and relaxing for my wee one, then I dip my fingers into it and massage it into the affected areas of the scalp. Really soak the flakes through, leaving them for as long as you can (for at least a couple of hours), and then, using a baby comb, a fine-tooth comb or your fingernails, gently scrape it off. It should lift away easily. Then reapply oil to the scalp and wash bub's head with a mild shampoo, as soap dissolves oil. Repeat as often as required.

Other itchy skin conditions. Porridge oats aren't just great for giving babies for breakfast, they also work well to soothe itchy skin or burns. Pop a cup (this isn't an exact measurement, I just mean a cup from the cupboard) of oats into a muslin and tie it up with a rubber band to form a pouch. Now run a shallow bath of warm water and throw that sucker in. Let it stew so the water becomes cloudy and then soak your child (of any age) in it for a while. It will relieve itching and prevent scarring.

I'm sure that you have a few old family wives' tales under your belt that really do work. It's worth tapping your family and friends, etc., for advice, as you will be surprised by the wealth of information and tips and tricks that have been passed down through the ages. You can always filter them to suit you, and maybe don't try the whisky in the milk one, but when it comes to baby knowledge and know-how, an oldie is generally a goodie.

Getting Attached

Whether it's their thumb, fingers, a dummy, a soft toy or a muslin, or curling or eating their hair, our wee ones can get attached to things, sometimes to the point of not being able to function without their particular comforter. I remember a windy, wet afternoon spent in a shopping centre car park hunting for my baby sister's well-worn bit of sheepskin rug that she could not live without. It was not located, and a tough night(s) was had by all until a new sheepskin rug had been bought and suitably 'broken in' to meet her standard. This bit of material had to smell right, feel right (worn down) and be the right size to hold. We practically had to bury it, wash it multiple times and run over it with the car before cutting it up. To this day, my sister still has 'sheepy' mark two. And she even got married with a small piece pinned to her bouquet to help calm her nerves.

This is every parents' nightmare, and dream, as when they do attach to something it helps them to feel calm and/or get to sleep. But when they do lose that special object, or the time comes for them to give it up, it can be the hardest thing in the world. However, the choices you make over your child's special attachment can be based on circumstances. Giving up sucking a thumb or a dummy is necessary for speech and tooth development, whether it's time to give up a pillowcase or doll, well, that's debatable.

Here's some tried and true advice on attaching and detaching.

Buy multiple. If it's a material (literally made of material) thing, say a blankie, doll or teddy, and you have found that it gets trailed everywhere, then it's best to invest in a few of them (one for the car, one for grandma's, etc.). There is nothing worse than when it gets mislaid and nothing else will do. I had one wee one that reluctantly agreed to let me wash her teddy every so often, but she would sit watching it in the washing machine and then wait right by the dryer for it to become available again – I couldn't hang it on the line, as it had to be ready as quickly as possible.

With the ease of Amazon and eBay nowadays, buying in a few or, in the worst-case scenario, a replacement, is easier (but it's best to have them in reserve, as finding that one teddy that went out of production and is now a collector's item can be expensive). I have found that you can switch them out for washing or repair. If it is a blanket and big enough, cutting it in half or more and edging the hem to make several mini favourite blankets is a great option, although my now 16-year-old tells me that the day he came home and found his blanket in quarters, all hemmed with blue satin ribbon (it was the ribbon he liked to hold onto while going to sleep rather than the actual blanket) still haunts him to this day. He is kidding (I hope), but the threadbare blanket was falling to pieces and thanks to me saving a piece, he still sleeps with it now (under his pillow, of course).

So as not to scar them for life, I've tried to encourage my wee ones, be it in a job or my own, to imprint on something more common than a blanket or teddy. My favourite, and theirs too, is a muslin. These are soft, available to bulk buy, and are easy to wash, find and carry. This was so successful for one family I worked for that I had to get individual mee-mees (what we called them) for the children, dying one pink and the other blue. (This choice wasn't based on gender, by the way, it's just that these two colours were the only ones that would hold.)

Set a time limit for when they should let their attachment go. This is only for things that will cause lasting effects if they don't give them up, such as sucking fingers, thumbs, a dummy or their hair. When I say sucking one's fingers can have a detrimental effect in later years, I am speaking from personal expense and experience. I had to have teeth removed and painful braces fitted in order to put my teeth back into place. I had pushed them so far out at the front that I could eat an apple through a tennis racket.

As soothing as sucking a thumb/finger can be, it can damage nail beds, hinder speech development and jaw growth, and cause teeth displacement. Sucking a dummy is not really any better, but although as parents we can nicely remove the dummy, the same can't be said for digits! Sucking on hair (this is usually in older children) can impact their stomach and bowels, as they can swallow the chewed hair, which then collects in the body. Some children even need to have these hairballs surgically removed.

But that's all the negatives, now here's how to counter them. The habit of sucking thumbs or fingers is the hardest to break, as it can start even in the womb, so try to direct them to finding comfort in other things. The aim of this is to help them gain the same feeling of security from that object instead. You may have to be a wee bit harsh and use a deterrent, such as gloves and/or nail varnish that tastes horrible. If you see them swaying relentlessly towards sucking their thumb, it might be best to introduce a dummy.

When you feel their time with a dummy has run its natural course, there are ways of removing it. The most effective way, I have found, is to phase it out. If they are spitting it out whilst asleep then that's a clear indication that they don't need it in order to sleep through the night. So, go in and either take it out of their mouth sooner or remove it from the bed once it's been discarded. Then don't provide it during daylight hours unless it's truly needed. I have found if they only have it as a bedtime binky it becomes easier to phase out.

You could always do what my sister did and scatter six dummies around the cot, before reducing the number over time, so they get used to sleeping without them. Or you could try my method, which is to tie the binky to the muslin, so my wee one can always reach around the cloth and find it in the night. On my last check in, I then untie it, in the hope she will be satisfied with just the feel of the muslin.

Most children want to feel grown up and in control of their lives, so when they are old enough to communicate with, and if they have a sibling on the way or know a smaller child, it's a good idea to encourage them to give their dummy away. I make a song and dance about rounding up the dummies and other baby things to pass on, and then I get the wee one to help me wrap them up. Making them part of the process is vital. We address the parcel to the Binky Fairies, other babies, Dummy Land – whatever works – and send it off. This is a way to honour the graduation of your child from baby to big person. They'll feel they have made the decision to do this, and with lots of encouragement and praise from you, the transition will be implanted in their minds.

Hair sucking is a different matter. I have found that whether they are partial to their own or yours, they do it more for stimulation than comfort. They seem to like the feel of the hair on their face. I got around this by giving the wee one a clean, unused but extremely soft make-up brush so she could stroke her face when she was feeling anxious. She had it in bed with her and it worked great, as her hand would get tired and she would fall asleep. She used to watch a movie before bedtime whilst stroking her face to relax. No more hair sucking!

For the aforementioned material things, such as teddies and blankets, I don't see why you need to remove these at all. In my experience, with a little positive encouragement from you, they will eventually opt to leave the said item behind or in bed to be snuggled later. They literally grow out of it on their own. Maybe I'm just saying all this because I still have my childhood teddy bear. He now sits watching over my wee one from the shelf. I find comfort in knowing he is now chasing away her nightmares.

Now for the science bit.

It all goes in the mouth. As pointed out above, most children grow out of their need to put something in their mouth or keep something close to it – you will find that they'll sleep with muslins/teddies close to their face. This phase of development only lasts so long. Freud coined it the 'oral stage' (which moves on to the aptly named 'anal stage'). The oral stage just means that everything has to be discovered through the mouth. Babies know that food comes to them that way, so they trust it. Milk and bottles equal life when they are little, so when they find new things, they want to experience them through their tongue. Every parent knows that everything goes in the mouth and gets licked, chewed and spat on, including us! But once they learn how to feel, see and suss items out by using their cognitive rather than their motor skills, this phase will pass. The anal phase is about them moving from us teaching them to discovering things for themselves, such as their bodies. Their brains are able to label things from sight and touch. Freud noticed how children went from being preoccupied with what went into their bodies to what came out of them. His terms, though antiquated today, do show that babies finding comfort in sucking or chewing things is deep seated in the brain and can be hard to replace. Every baby will do it and eventually grow out of it. So, when they say it's just a phase, they mean it.

In addition, sucking on something is a natural predilection for babies, hence the suckle instinct when feeding during those first six months, be it from a bottle or breast. So, if you can introduce something for them to attach to and suck in times of need, you are encouraging this natural suck and swallow reflex and reducing the risk of Sudden Infant Death Syndrome (SIDS) in the process.

Aside from this, there are several schools of thought on oral aids for babies. In writing these blogs, I have found both pros and cons for babies having something to suck on to help them settle that isn't you or held by you. I'll be honest, I was one of those nannies then mums who didn't like dummies. As a nanny, I worked hard to discourage my charges from using one, and their mums usually agreed with this approach. I actively encouraged my babies to imprint on a material item instead. Then my child came along, and my husband gave her a dummy when I wasn't looking. I had to respect his input in raising her. I don't know if she would have slept through the night so soon without one, but her restful nights meant ours were, too, so they can't all be bad. But my daughter did imprint on a soft toy called 'Ippo the Hippo' as well. I'm hoping that when the time comes, having this special friend will help her to leave her binky behind.

Whatever your feelings on oral pacifiers, there is no right or wrong, just go with whatever works for you . . . no judgements and no guilt. My only rule for an oral settling aid is that it does need to be phased out or removed cold turkey (again, whatever works for you), because in older children it can cause mouth ulcers and the over production of saliva, which gives them a painful chin rash and cracked lips, not to mention (again) causes speech impairment and jaw misalignment.

Forming attachments and finding comfort in something is a good thing. We do it right from the womb, sucking our thumbs or holding our own hands and umbilical cord. Once we are out, we need and find familiarity and safety in the smell, touch or taste of something. So, that might mean Mummy giving her t-shirt to Daddy when she wants him to take over the night shift. In order for my daughter to get to sleep, she needs music, a familiar muslin and, at the moment anyway, her dummy (which I'm phasing out as her teeth are coming in). The world is a wonderful but overwhelming place for our wee ones. Every moment of the day, they are being bombarded with experiences and assaults on their senses, which they then need to sort out through the night. So, I would not deny them the chance to find peace and comfort in something constant and familiar in any way. It's completely up to you and your family what that special thing is – a soft toy, a treasured t-shirt or, like Linus Van Pelt from the *Peanuts* comic strip, a blanket – and for how long they have it. We all need our home comforts.

Get on the Floor

One of the things I loved as a nanny was getting down to it. Getting on the floor and in the sand or mud. I'd get right into my wee one's world and experience it through them. As a nanny, I was expected to get into everything. I was paid to play, to interact and to interpret their world. Now, as a parent, I know it really is the best way to have a rewarding relationship with your little one.

Right from the moment you are happy to pop them on the floor (as my gran used to say, they can't fall off the floor), you should be down there, too, playing with the toys and interacting with your baby. There should be lots of eye contact and touching, as you show them how the toys work. Sing and talk about whatever comes to mind. Heck, you could even just tell them about your day. Just get down there and get stuck in. Sometimes, needs must and we do have to pop them down while we wander off to get something done. That's great, but we must also be aware that when we are in the room with them, it's good not to crouch over them. I am an advocate for self-play. I may be wrong but allowing your kids to learn to entertain themselves is a very important skill, as you are not always there, and neither should you be. However, I am also an advocate for getting involved whenever you can. Learning to play with others and interact is also a wonderful life skill that starts from an early age.

If you can get into the habit of seeing the world from their point of view, it will have so many benefits for later years. Getting down and sitting on the floor allows them to talk to you face to face. They learn from watching you talk and how you move and vocalise. It is a wonderful way to encourage them to trust in you, and to feel they can talk to you. Having an open channel of communication even at this young age is vital.

Getting down to their level or bringing them up to yours (I used to sit a wee one on the bench with me, if they were able to support themselves) allows them to interact directly with you. (In addition, putting them on something saves your back.) Adults, especially tall ones, can be very daunting to small children. Even if you are their parents, by coming down to their level, you are literally taking away the distance between you. Toddlers especially will hang off your leg at the most inopportune times for support (physical and emotional), so giving them a level playing field can help with the dreaded whining and grizzling for attention.

I definitely feel that getting down on the floor helps a child to feel acknowledged and safe, as they stride out on their own, widening their horizons and boundaries both inside and outside the home. If they know they have a safe space with you, they will be more adventurous and confident and take more chances in their learning experience, as they copy what they see. I am not suggesting you crawl around down there always. Trust me, that's not helping anyone. When they are really small, try putting them up high in a bouncer on the kitchen table, where they will be able to see and interact with you. When they are older, lie on the floor facing the ceiling and play with hands and feet; yours and theirs. Once they are sitting, getting close can help with learning body parts; head, shoulders, knees and toes can only be explored face to face! Once they are independent, don't be afraid to get into the sand with them. Make mud pies and build the towers for them to knock over. We can get so caught up in our own lives sometimes that we don't realise the impact that sitting on the couch or being up high and literally talking down to our kids can have. If you are going to check your phone, sit on the floor and let them remind you to pay attention to them by trying to take it off you! Playing with your child has been shown to increase development in language, social skills, cognitive development and gross motor skills. However, I do love to sit back and watch them interpret an object – maybe a drum needs to be taste tested first and then hit with heels not hands. It's wonderful to see how they want the world to be.

Remember, everything they do will one day be for the last time, so enjoy the limited moments you have to do these things with your child. The time passes too fast, and one day soon they will be on the couch with their phones ignoring you.

Up, Up and Away

So, she has done it! She has taken the first tentative steps to being a toddler and is crawling. I could have just as easily said walking, as some babies are on their feet by eight months, and this is kind of what this blog is about – how quickly they can move along the steppingstones and how we as parents need to move faster. Once they are crawling, they get a taste for it and everything is an adventure. It's all, 'I can get there, oh, what's over there? I know, I'll follow Mummy to the kitchen, to the washing line and the loo!' This is wonderful, but all these wee paths are full of dangers that we don't notice, as they are not on our level, but need to because they are on theirs. And we need to think a couple of levels up, too, as once they're crawling, it'll be no time at all before they're pulling up and walking away. These are all wonderful steps to witness, but as a nanny, my brain is hardwired to see the trip hazards, quite literally!

Here are a few must dos:

Fireguard. If you have a fire, open or gas, it needs to be covered, not only for safety, but it will save a lot of cleaning when they get into the soot.

Knick knacks. Find them an alternative home for now. If you think they can't reach something, they can! Everything goes up (the rule of thumb is their height plus an arm reach. Go higher as they learn to climb).

Cupboard doors, on everything. Our wee ones are stronger than you think, and they are also determined. If they see you open and close a cupboard door, they'll want in. There are some great locks out there that can go inside the cupboard door, out of sight, and simple ones that bar the handles. Whatever your décor, you should be able to find something to suit.

Stairs. This is a no brainer when they are wee and just starting out, as stairs will become the ultimate goal – they'll want to go up in the world. So, get a gate (you can get screw in or tension ones), preferably one for the top and the bottom of the stairs. (I put one at the top once they are walking.) I also make a huge effort every day to get them to go up and down the stairs (ensuring they always go down backwards and under supervision). This avoids you having to carry them up and down all the time, and it's great for their confidence and muscles . . . for bubs, it's a bit like climbing a mountain.

Blind cords. When I was a nanny, I heard of a little one who tragically died after getting herself caught up in a blind cord, so check whether yours will be in reaching distance. I have a plastic clip that screws to the wall, which the cords can be tucked into, ensuring that nothing is hanging down to ensnare wee ones. In the past, I have also thrown my curtain cords up and over the railings. There are many options to research on the internet for securing your cords. If you have them, just remember to tie them up and keep them out of the way.

Radiators. This is a personal preference depending on how hot you have them, and if you wish to simply educate them about hot and not (as in don't touch), but if the heat concerns you, you can get covers to fit all types of radiator, and they're generally not too expensive.

Cabinets. This is a big one, as wee ones climb and will scale anything and everything they can. There are clips that you can fix to the wall to secure your chest of drawers and bookcases. Early on in my career, I saw a set of drawers go over on a baby (it was lightweight and relatively empty, so no harm was done, but a big lesson was learnt), so I am only too aware of the dangers. If your drawers are full, make sure they are securely shut. There are many options to research online that will help you do this, from child-safe stick-on clips to screw in or magnetic openers.

TV. As with cabinets, these can go over, so fix yours to the wall or high up out of bub's reach. There are great brackets available that fix to the wall and pivot, so you can move the TV to suit the audience and push it back to the wall when it's not in use. Also, use cable covers to keep all the hanging wires that attach to our many boxes and gadgets together, so they won't be enticing to our little people.

Cords/cables. This one is also a no brainer, as they are on the floor, which is your baby's domain. So, hide them or move them out of reach. Alternatively, invest in some cord covers, which are large tubes that you can put all the cables in. Lamps, radio cords and anything that plugs in, especially night lights and monitors in the wee one's rooms, need to be well covered and hidden away.

All this is great for the first couple of months of movement, but in the end, you will want your house back, and not everywhere you go will be baby proofed. If you only went places that were safe, you might never leave the house. So, when their language has started to develop, you can start to educate them about being safe in their world. They need to learn boundaries and rules. Knickknacks can come back with instructions not to touch or use them as a toy. (But if the ornament is very dear to you, best to keep it in a safe place.) Fires can be uncovered and with supervision enjoyed safely. Stairs can be ungated, etc., and cabinets unlocked (except the ones containing medicine and cleaning products, which should always be kept locked away or, even better, high out of reach).

This brings me nicely to my next suggestion. All this putting away of stuff and telling them 'no' and 'don't touch' can seem negative, so make sure that your wee one has a space that is all theirs. Provide them with a toy box that they can tip out and tidy up on their own, and/or a space in which to spread out. I have an unlocked cupboard in the kitchen that is full of things they can play with; a silicone spatula and mixing bowls, old Tupperware that is missing the lids, a few toys, a saucepan, some wooden spoons and some boxes (kids and cats love boxes!). While we are occupying the kitchen, bubs knows this is her cupboard to empty out, stack stuff up, knock stuff over and make a mess. She also knows that she needs to put everything away again, which she seems to love to do. I encourage it wholeheartedly.

Knowing where to start when it comes to baby proofing can seem daunting. I guess it's the nanny in me, but I am one to err on the side of caution. I will be safe rather than sorry until I can communicate with my wee one and she can navigate the house safely and securely.

Grumpy Guts

My wee one is on the move. Well, kind of. She is crawling like a G.I. Joe right now. Combining that with a roll from her back to her tummy, she is getting around the place, just not fast enough (for her, I'm fine with the slow progress). She wants to go, mostly to finally catch the cats, I think, but yes, through steely determination and a war cry of frustration, she is getting ready to become mobile. Her bum is up and her knees are poised, only her front half seems not to get the message, so, by the time it joins the party, her bum has collapsed and she takes to inchworming it around the place. It's very cute to watch from our end, but, boy, does she get frustrated, telling everyone in the vicinity, including the neighbours, all about it. This coupled with two front teeth erupting from her gums means she is a Grumpy Guts. Now, as I am not from around these parts, I don't know if you use this term? For me, it means fed up, frustrated and in pain of some sort.

Every child goes through this, a lot, until they can logically figure things out. But then again, I have been accused of displaying the symptoms of a Grumpy Guts sometimes in my adult life, too! Anyway, they will whine, cry (half-heartedly), yell, put their head face down on the floor and then look to you to help them. They want to be held, touched and be able to see you. They want to be picked up, put down, not touched and get going all at the same time. In short, they know what they want, they just don't know how or what to do to get it. This is where you can help.

Give them lots of praise, whether they're crawling, eating and sitting up (or whatever they are trying to do). Make sure you give them the right encouraging noises ('cos that's all life's about for them right now). Give them lots of 'yahoos' and 'good girl/boy'. Higher-pitched voices will instil excitement in them. It gives them a lift and releases endorphins in their brain, and they will want to have that feeling again.

Get in their face and smile and make eye contact. Get on their level, whether that be on the floor or at the table, and clap, punch the air or wave your hands around. Let them know that you think they are on the right track. Also, do what they are trying to do, so they can copy you. For babies, learning is part brain reaction – they get an urge to crawl, etc. – and part copying. They want to do what you do, whether that's feeding themselves, picking up their toy or sitting on the floor.

Get physical. You can help with exercising their bodies in a way that stimulates muscle memory and cognitive development. Cross patterning involves doing exercises with your baby to 'switch' their brain on – in other words, it's the act of crossing the body's centre line to engage the opposing sides of the brain. Our left side controls the right, and vice versa, so they work together and coordinate. The best way to help them is to sing songs to them while touching their opposite feet to their opposite hands. While they are on their backs after a bath or during a nappy change, encourage them to cross the centre line and touch their toes to the opposite finger, toes to nose. Rotate their hips and massage their joints, stretching their limbs out and unfolding them. To help them with crawling, while they're on their backs, push their knees up to their tummies and go through the motions. This will help them to get to know the feel of the movement, which they will then try to replicate when they are on the floor.

Grumpy Guts is just the pure frustration of there being a difference between what they want to do and what they can do, so helping them and getting involved in their journey will lessen the time they spend feeling at odds with the world. Let them know you are their support crew and cheerleader all rolled into one. You will catch them and pop them back on the right track, be that physically or mentally. From the get-go, communication in both of these fields is important for you and your baby. They need to know you are there for them and, therefore, are safe to explore and taste and try out their world. You need to support them, but you also need to just let them go through it, as it will provide the motivation to take that next leap. Don't pick them up instantly, let them grizzle but get over to you. If they are trying to feed themselves, let them; it's messy, but they will get it. The feeling of achievement when they do get something is also what will motivate them to try again at what they haven't quite mastered, whether that's sitting up, using a spoon or walking. We need to be there as a safety net until they learn to do it on their own.

So, let them turn into a Grumpy Guts, as it'll all be worth it in the end.

Chatterbox, talking Motherese

I've written a few posts on talking, you to your baby and your baby to you, stressing the importance of both chatting to them and encouraging them to chat to you. As I've said many times, it's not English in those first few months of communication, but they still all seem to have a lot to say! However, this piece is dedicated to my hubby, who said to me today that I was using a baby voice and asked why I was talking to our child in this manner? He felt it was not needed, so let me create the scene and set the record straight. I was giving our wee one a 'polish' after our shower. She loves getting in with me, but that's for another blog. A polish is a vigorous rub down with a towel that leaves the wee one dry and in fits of giggles. While I was doing this, I told her how beautiful all her body parts were to me as I dried them. I kissed her tummy and did some raspberries, which brought on another fit of giggles. I did this all in a sing-song voice (high-pitched but soft, usually with rhyme in the lexicon, tosey wosey, etc.). It's this that Hubby had the problem with. But we change our tone with babies pretty much instinctively, and it's been proven that our natural predilection to do this is right on the money. So, ignore my husband and I'll tell you why – and how you should talk to your little one.

You naturally sing softly to your child from the day they are born, be it a hum in your chest to reassure them or to help them to sleep, with music at a group or in the car, or in the house while counting their fingers and toes. You automatically raise your pitch when you talk to them to match the leap in your heart that you feel when you see them. This is all a language of love, which is known as Motherese and is officially recognised as a form of communication. When you talk to your baby in a higher-pitched cadence, it switches on their brainwaves and syncs with your voice, allowing them to make connections and kickstart learning. The word Motherese was coined by scientists at Cambridge University, who found that the more babies heard their mothers speak at this pitch, the better their language development. So, our cutesy voice is exactly what we should be using to communicate with our wee ones right from the get-go.

Nursery rhymes are the best and easiest way to use this sing-song language with your baby. Repeating lines over and over will create ear worms for both of you. You will remember them being sung to you and notice that most have a very similar pattern when it comes to the tune and words, as well as repeating verses that are easy to remember. When you repeat lines and tunes, this stimulates all parts of your child's brain and helps the development of their cognitive and gross motor skills. If this is your first child, I recommend signing up for a class that is either paid for or free and learning all the staple nursery rhymes so you can sing them at home. This will also mean you won't look so silly to strangers in the park, as you'll be singing actual songs rather than the weather forecast. But, as I have no shame and am aware of the importance of Motherese for my baby, I try to use it in all my verbal transactions with her, wherever we happen to be.

Motherese isn't just a language for mums, although in the first few months babies respond better to their mother's voice. Anyone interacting with your child on a regular basis, including carers, grandparents and especially dads, should use this way of talking to them. It is science, but not rocket science. When your baby is that cute, it brings out that sort of way of talking to them anyway, so just go with it. You can be safe in the knowledge that you are doing exactly the right thing for their cognitive development and speech.

Once you show babies how, you will notice an increase in noises and babbling, which usually occurs around the same time as weaning. This is because they are learning how to use their mouths and are developing an appreciation, of course, for all the lovely tastes and textures you are providing for them. Suddenly, life doesn't comprise solely of a liquid diet and tongue development, chewing movements and jaw maturity and control all come into play. They will find they are able to open and close their mouths, and that their muscles remember exactly how to do so. And boy, do they love practising this. This won't happen just by them spitting food out. They will start to sing to themselves, too, desperately mimicking you. And in the case of a friend of mine's baby, loudly and very high-pitched (think Mariah Carey as an infant). They are exercising their vocal cords and stretching their range from the simple communication of crying. My wee one grumbles and growls during mealtimes, going up high and down low as she attempts to find the right pitch.

Your little one will start to have conversations with other babies (it's so funny to see)! Lie them together and they will chat up a storm like nattering old ladies. They will also start to focus in on conversations that you are having and join in, looking directly at you and babbling, usually at nappy times when your faces are very close. This is what you want! Jump in and chat back. You can either fill in the gap with English (or your chosen language, and yes, if there is a chance of them learning two then go for it) and/or copy them with baby babble. Encourage them to speak up and out. It is proven that children who are spoken to directly, and included in conversations going on around them, such as at the dinner table (have them eat with you at the same time), have a much wider and varied vocabulary and speak sooner (hmmm, that might not be the best thing – just kidding!). They learn faster and their brain develops better than if they have been educated mostly by the TV. But don't get me wrong, there are some wonderful programmes now that have looked at early sounds and incorporated them into their show to directly encourage speech development (the BBC is very good: *In the Night Garden* and *Teletubbies*, etc.). What sounds like babble is exactly that and children respond to repetition and gobbledygook. (In other words, they will engage by using their own language and trying to echo the sounds they hear.)

Play, play play. Get down onto the floor and interact with them, talking your time as you do so. "Red blocks, oh, look, I'm stacking them. Look, this fits in here. Wow, what's this puppet doing?" Give a running narrative to their day and then breathe, allowing them to learn about the pauses in conversations. Let them speak out and give them a lot of praise when they do. Soon, the sounds will start to be recognisable as the language you speak. (If you're going bilingual don't panic, they will be 'slower' to speak, which is completely normal – you would be too if you were processing two different phonics.)

Once they are older and starting to speak, incorporate some corrections. When they do start to copy you and begin talking, they won't get it right the first time. But you need to encourage them in every way with lots of praise, be it in the form of a smile, a yahoo, a clap, a pat on the back or cheerleader moves (I have been known to throw some shapes in the privacy of my own home). And correct them at the same time. Say the word they are trying to say the right way. As cute as their pronunciation is, they will continue to get it wrong if you don't put them right. They are looking to you to lead them.

For example, my wee one is fascinated with shoes. It comes out fuze. Now, I know she's trying to say shoes, as she is handing them to me at the same time. It is wonderful watching her brain work. She knows she's not saying it quite right and tries many times. I help by saying 'shhhhhhoooes' over and over, allowing her to hear the letters. She will get it. But I have to be careful not to mimic her and instead get her to copy me, as she will start calling them fuze if I don't gently correct her.

This is a wonderful time, when you see the light bulbs going off and lighting up their faces: "I know this one, I can wave, or do the actions", and they will start to attempt to make the words or sounds that accompany life. And the pride in your eyes when they see that they are on the right track is priceless. I am looking forward to the things that my little one will begin to say . . .

Fists of fury

It's started; her lip starts to tremble, she looks at me accusingly, stamps her feet and unleashes the fists of fury. The volume and intensity escalate, and we are off. This is a tantrum; they all have them and they're nothing to be afraid of, embarrassed by or something to feel guilty about. No one has done anything wrong. Tantrums are simply an expression of an emotion that they can't tell you about, so instead they show you. Usually, they happen because things aren't going their way or as they planned. They can be triggered by any of the following:

» They don't like what's happening

» You're not paying them enough attention

» They are tired/hungry/frustrated/hurt

» They are not feeling in control of a situation

» They are feeling scared/insecure

» You're not picking up their non-verbal communications

» Their emotional or physical needs are not being met

» Or it could be that you gave them the wrong-coloured cup or made them wear pants on a Tuesday!

Tantrums start a lot earlier then you probably imagined they would, and they go on for a lot longer than you want. But don't lose hope, as there are ways of minimising them. Once you have understood the root of the problem, you can help your child calm down.

Here are a few ways to determine what's bugging them.

Make an effort to pick up on non-verbal clues. My wee one is fourteen months old and very independent and headstrong. She knows what she wants and is trying hard to tell me, but she's not speaking yet so I miss some of her cues. I have to make a conscious effort to read her, so that she doesn't end up having a meltdown. For example, at the swimming pool today, she was desperate to get out of the water. She kept repeatedly climbing out and trying to get to the changing rooms. Every time I brought her back to the pool, she started crying. I reasoned that having come all this way, she should jolly well do some swimming, only to later find out that she had pooped. As soon as I had cleaned her up, she wanted to get back in the water. This was a lesson for me; she had been trying to tell me something, but as I hadn't understood her, she had cried as a final act of desperation. I now know I need to look at situations closer and see if I can figure out what she needs versus what I want or think she wants.

Wants and needs. As I've explained, tantrums are usually their final resort to getting the attention they need. At the same time, parents need to be aware that they're pretty fast learners and will soon work out that by throwing a wobbly they can get the attention they crave. We need to learn how to separate the two. We all know the difference between a want and a need, i.e., I need you to feed me versus I want that food. The same goes for toys, your attention, etc. It's your job to work out whether they need or want it. If they are trying to get something they need, we need to help make that happen for them. If they are trying for something they want, we need to figure out whether it is really necessary. Understanding these subtle differences can help ease frustration on everybody's part. If they need something, you will hopefully be able to provide it, if they don't then there are ways of sidestepping the landmine that is a brewing tantrum.

How to do this.

Listen to their cries. This is really important, as their cry is their way of letting you know what they want. Is the cry a yell or a shout, or is it angry, long and whiny? If the answer is yes, then they don't need what they want. This will be shown in their verbal and non-verbal communication (such as hanging off your leg). And this can be draining for everyone. They are simply bored and hoping you will entertain them, and usually at the worst possible times – it happens around dinnertime for my wee one. Listen out for whether it's a true cry or a grizzle. Trust me, you will know the difference instinctively, and then you can act accordingly.

Without *giving in* to her, I've found that giving five minutes of my time and acknowledging her can get me fifteen minutes of doing what I need to do in relative peace and quiet. When I'm preparing meals, my wee one, who is usually extremely independent, will all of a sudden need to cling to my leg and grizzle. I have found that at these moments, I need to put the prep to one side and sit on the floor with her, so that I'm on her level. I recognise that she just wants to know what's going on and to feel involved. Even when she doesn't want to play with me during the day, she wants to know that I'm available to her. When I'm busy cooking, I have my back to her, and it's this that seems to set her off. So, I either get on the floor with her for a few minutes or get her set up with an activity, such as reading a book or doing a puzzle. Sometimes, I get her to go in her ball pit, as it takes her a few minutes to get out again! Or I pop on some music and we dance around the kitchen. This way, I'm involving her in something and distracting her, leaving me free to nip back to the chopping board while she's throwing some moves. Recently, I have started putting a chair up to the kitchen top so she can stand and watch me. As soon as she's old enough, I will get her to help. This both engages *and* teaches her. She's also learning that while she's got me to notice her, she hasn't got my full-on attention just because she is grizzling. But by acknowledging her, it's easier to sidestep a tantrum. Once she is older, I will be tougher, as I will use communication to convey that she needs to entertain herself while I'm busy. We will talk, and she'll learn that I can't drop everything on her whim.

But if the cry is real and pulls at your heartstrings, etc., then they have a need that is not being met. Usually this is about them feeling insecure or not in control. This is when you need to step in and help them figure the problem out. Your wee one is looking for your help. You can provide this by stepping in and leading them to safety, either physical or mental. You may need to show them a different way of doing things or scoop them into your arms to restore their confidence that they can do whatever it is that's perplexing them to meltdown proportions.

As they cry, are they looking over at you to see if you're watching? If they are then this one is a just-for-attention tantrum, and I find it best to ignore it and them. If you run over/stop what you're doing, you are just teaching them that to get their way all they have to do is fake it. In these situations, I find it best to verbally acknowledge them. Say their name over and over in a bright, happy voice. Make eye contact but don't get on the floor with them, as for this one, you really don't want to be stooping to their level.

Can you distract them with something to stop them from crying? Until the time comes when you can sit down with them and orchestrate a dialogue, I've found that coming up with an alternative is an effective approach. Giving them sweets isn't really appropriate, but you could let them have some fruit. If you're going round the supermarket and they've seen something they want that you don't want to give them, you could try getting them to hold your shopping list or carry some of the food from your basket or trolley, which will keep them occupied. If it's a toy they're after that isn't available, try distracting them with another. Simply giving them a hug will be enough to help them feel secure before they trundle off to the next thing.

Stand your ground. This is Behaviour 101 for your child. They are learning boundaries within themselves, their peers, their family and in the outside world. Try to establish what your own boundaries are first, and then stand your ground when it comes to them. Everyone has their own family rules and lines which must not be crossed. Talking to other mums, I find it funny how they always seem to default to the rules they hated as a child. "I swear I will never do that!" suddenly becomes, "I swear by that!" As a kid, my step-mum didn't allow me to walk around with food. I could never see the point in obeying this rule, much to her frustration. Now I'm a stickler for it with my wee one. I'm always telling her to sit down. Being consistent is vital. If you say one thing one day and not the next, you're giving them mixed signals and failing to establish boundaries. They don't know what's what and this can cause them to have tantrums. It's a bit like routine, they like to know what's happening in their world so they can be secure in moving through it.

Try to pre-empt a meltdown by using your mindreading skills. I know this can't always be done, but when they can't communicate, try to be like a concierge in a hotel and meet their needs, wants and desires before they even know they have them. For instance, have a snack ready before their blood sugar dips, pop them into bed for their nap before they've even started to rub their eyes or feel a lapse in concentration. Orchestrate activities, such as letting them run around the garden when they have energy to burn, and have a few books on hand for when they need a rest stop. I have found that if you cover all the bases you can get through your day nicely, without any wee blips, as their needs and wants are being met. Therefore, they won't need to misbehave or try to get your attention. (Actually, I don't like the word misbehave when referring to a wee one. They are not deliberately trying to annoy you, they are just acting on what they know/feel at any given moment. Trust me, I have teens and I would take a toddler tantrum over a chip-on-shoulder/entitled teenager ANY day.)

But sometimes nothing is right and nothing you can do will fix it, as they don't actually know what is wrong, either. There is just something, and it gets blown out of all proportion. When – not if – this happens, you need to do and remember a few things.

Never tell them off. They are just communicating with you, and by getting angry you will only make things worse. Telling them they are being silly belittles their feelings and emotions. Everyone gets frustrated at times, and they are just exercising that in the only way they know how.

Find a safe space. Sometimes, a tantrum can get physical, involving body thrashing, kicking, running away and punching. For your safety and theirs, and wherever you happen to be, find a corner so they can get it out of their system. NO parent is ever going to judge you, and forget anyone who gives you a dirty look – they clearly don't have kids!

Let it play out. If it's safe to turn your back on them when they are playing up, then do so. I know this seems harsh, but there is no talking them down. Tantrums are like storms, they might get worse for a while, but they will literally blow themselves out.

Calm down. Once they have started to settle down, give them some reassurance, as they are not being naughty, they're just frustrated. Give them some physical or verbal cues that you're not going to give in, but that you still love them, and then hopefully you can both move on. When they are older, they will sometimes feel embarrassed over an outburst, and if you make an example of them you can make that worse.

Tantrums happen when communication has got lost in translation. So, we as parents need to make sure that we set good boundaries while allowing them choices, so they feel in control of their world. For example, if they want juice, but they've already had some, offer them milk or water instead. They might still really want juice, but by giving them a choice they won't feel you're putting your will on them (even though you are). As much as possible, try to plan your day. For example, don't go shopping when they are tired or hungry, and that goes for you, too! If they've got a play date, factor in some sleep time in the car either before or afterwards. Always have some healthy snacks on your person, for when their blood sugar dips during the day. Carry a comfort item, such as a muslin, with you, so that in situations where they feel insecure they have a cape of strength to hand. Trust me, when children are happy, secure, fed and rested (just like us), tantrums can be contained and sometimes even defused.

By looking out for and picking up their cues, by listening to what they need and want, by thinking of things to distract them with and by doing a little forward planning, tantrums don't have to be scary things that are upsetting and humiliating for all involved. They are part of life, and with communication, acknowledgement and knowledge on your part, they can be a small phase rather than a big deal.

Get Them Some Exposure

Back when I was a nanny in London, one of the city's leading allergy specialists told me that while over-protective parents are great for business, we have to let our kids get dirty. In order to stop allergies from forming – I'm not talking here about the ones they may be born with, such as being allergic to bee stings, peanuts or having asthma, but the more everyday ones, such as to fur and pollen – we need to let them crawl around in nature and muck.

Here are some ideas so you will see where I am going with this . . .

When summer arrives, get outside. The sunshine season may only last a few days, but it's the ideal time for both you and your baby to top up your Vitamin D levels. When I moved to Ireland, I was told to give bubs supplements to make up for the lack of sunshine. This was an alien concept for me, as in New Zealand, we are told to get out of the sun, not to actively run towards it! But no Northern Hemisphere country gets enough sun time, and as a result we are often lacking in Vitamin D (which in some cases leads to brittle bones, delayed motor skills and weak muscles, as the sun and/or supplements help a growing body to absorb calcium). So, say yes to supplements and an even bigger yes to getting outside. I still advocate Slip-Slop-Slap (t-shirt, sun cream, hat), but get some skin time in as well (a few minutes a day without coverage to expose your own and bub's skin directly to the sunlight). Then pop the sun cream on, especially on the bottoms of their feet. My wee one is crawling, so the soles of her feet are exposed all the time, and I don't want her having burnt tootsies. Rumour has it that in order for you to absorb the vitamins your body needs, you should expose some of your skin to the sun for a stretch of 15 mins per day without cream.

Get on the grass. When babies are beginning to experience their world, they also need to be exposed *to* their world, so let them touch as much of it as they can. Heck, even let them roll around in some hay if you can find it. Take their shoes off and let them get dirty in the soil, crawl along the garden path and feel the grass between their toes. You can even stick flowers on their nose. All of this is fun, but at the same time it will be building up their resilience to grass spores, pollen and pollutants in the soil that come from pollutions in the rain. In addition, once your baby is old enough (over a year) introduce honey to their diet – and all the better if you can find local honey from bees in your area. Honey has so many medicinal properties, it's high in antioxidants and contains antiseptic and antibacterials. I'd argue it's close to a miracle cure. On its own, just a spoonful can soothe most minor illnesses, such as coughs and colds. Mixed with garlic, it is great for digestion and, most importantly, immunity. It's also rather lovely on toast. After all, how can Winnie the Pooh be wrong?

Pet everything. If you have pets, don't shy away from letting your child help provide care and cuddles. Don't worry too much about the cat hair on the couch and the dog scratching themselves next to the baby. Let them bury their hands and faces right in their fur. Exposure like this is invaluable to building up immunities and side-stepping the allergies and breathing problems associated with animal fur/pelt/hair. Once they are big enough, get them to a petting farm or zoo and let them touch all the lambs, bunnies and horses, etc. Wash their hands afterwards but remember that exposure is key.

Forget about the dusting! Another allergy on the rise is to dust. Some people are being too clean, and I figure they must have help, as I constantly feel that I'm fighting a losing battle with the housework. I try, but not too much, as exposure to dust is good for the body. Breathing in all the skin flakes and dirt particles for a bit (not constantly) will help to build up resistance in the wee one's lungs. So, I hereby give you permission not to over clean. It turns out that letting them crawl around on the floor and get their hands into everything is good for them and good for mummy, as that's the 20 minutes you were going to spend cleaning given over to relaxing.

Give them peanut butter. Even if there is an allergy in the family, it may not have been passed down. The best way to help your wee one taste it and see if it is a problem is to first put some on their skin. This is called a patch test. Then, if there's no welt or reaction, pop a wee bit on the inside of their lip. Wait and see, and if there's no reaction again, slather it on hot toast and away you go. Of course, if you are worried and/or there is a family history, have your GP run the patch and lip test in their surgery, where there will be help at hand in the unlikely event they do suffer a reaction. One of the kids I looked after when I was a nanny used an EpiPen, as she was allergic to tree nuts (pistachios and cashews), which is how I met the aforementioned allergy specialist. He told us to keep her eating as much mango and papaya as possible, as they are the cousins of tree nuts and would help build up her immunity. She did get a wee red rash on her mouth, but the doctor said her body would eventually balance out. It did, and six years later she is undergoing tests to see if she has outgrown the nut allergy too.

Eggs and dairy. This one needs to be done by trial and error, as unless there is a family history, you never know if your baby's digestive system is going to accept other animal products. If you think about it, we are drinking another mammal's milk, which is designed for another type of young. When we've finished breastfeeding, we don't continue to produce milk and give it to the cat. So, it is easy to understand why people's stomachs can be a bit funny when it comes to cow's milk. I advise slowly introducing it to your baby's diet, maybe in porridge and cereal and then later in yoghurts and cheese, etc., but serve each one separately, so as not to overload their system and so you can see if there is an intolerance.

Eggs are touch and go. There was one toddler in my care who was 18 months before her mum decided to give her eggs. She had one bite of an omelette and we were in A&E, as she had a very quick and violent reaction to the eggs. Her mum and I had to quickly learn to make egg-free recipes and baked goods. As with peanut butter, try a patch test first then give them a wee bite. Don't introduce any new foods for a week, so if there is a reaction, you will know immediately. Thankfully, there are dairy alternatives.

I recommend reintroducing any proteins, grains or dairy, as well as any fruits or vegetables that they have had a minor reaction to, and doing this slowly over time. Then just see how it goes. Children with continued exposure to irritations can build up tolerances and literally grow out of an allergy.

Mud pies. If you haven't made a mud pie, you're missing out and need to try this activity with your kids. There are even people out there who, for a reasonable price, will make you a mud kitchen out of palettes. Whether it's winter or summer, get some dirt, throw it into an old saucepan, add some water and mix it all together with a wooden spoon. This will give your wee ones of any age a wonderful, muddy activity in which to create, get mucky and expose themselves to all sorts of nasties that can then be washed away with a hot bath or a hose down.

Sandpits are also lots of fun, whether they're at the beach or a playground, or you have one in your own garden. You can bury your feet, build cities in the sand or just let it run between your fingers. Do be aware that sandpits are full of germs, lovely germs, which pass easily between kids. Things like threadworms lay their eggs on the sand, which then get transferred to a wee one's tummy, causing an itchy bottom. This is all good childhood fun and, a bit like nits, your child is unlikely to escape threadworms. And like nits, there will be lots of good remedies available in your local pharmacy to deal with any symptoms. To try and prevent this issue arising in the first place, invest in a cover for a private sandpit and wash their hands, especially under their nails, when they've finished playing.

Sharing spit. Unless you wash your toys before and after every play date and muzzle your child wherever they go, sharing spit with other children is inevitable. But this is good; kids pick up colds, coughs and rashes from the bodily fluids of their little friends and this is invaluable in building up their immune system, which will effectively see them through to adulthood. And as with shots, actually getting some of these rashes and minor ailments can help them to not get worse ones. Avoiding chicken pox and measles and mumps, etc., when you are a child and then getting sick with them as an adult (if you haven't had a jab) can be extremely uncomfortable and even life threatening. While I was looking after a brother and sister many moons ago, I phoned up the school to say they would not be in due to chickenpox. Within hours, every one of their friends' mums had called asking if they could expose their child to mine so they could get it and get it out of the way. We ended up having a chickenpox party. My kids sucked on twenty lollipops and handed them out. Whole classes of kids got a milder strain of the infection. They had a few days off school and Bob was our uncle!

I know that us mums are often in two minds between keeping our kids germ free and clean and trying to give them a fighting chance of not becoming allergic to everything. It's difficult to know whether to allow them to get sick or to shield them to stay well. I say let them get down and dirty while you wait in the wings with a wet cloth until their play or day comes to an end. Let them get the bugs, and in turn the resistance, but provide them with some tender loving care and medicine when they do feel under the weather. This will give them the best of both worlds.

Ahead of the Class

I now live in a smaller part of the world, where life is not as hectic, fast-paced and cutthroat. I nannied for years in London, where the childrearing world could get extremely competitive. Trust me, you had to go to the right classes, enrol them in the right preschool and school, join the right clubs and be invited to the right houses.

The families I worked with were all different, and it was interesting to go from job to job getting to know their different outlooks for what they wanted for their kids. But the school thing wasn't just about being seen at the right gates, it was about the ever-increasing population and actually getting a place at any school. No matter what socioeconomic bracket you fall into, there is competition to get a school place. It hits our news every year that children are having to travel miles to a school because the one on the corner is full. It's a preoccupation for parents everywhere, as is ensuring they attend all the open days for their chosen schools and getting information on feeder preschools, etc. (Feeder preschools are ones with direct links and automatic enrolment to a primary school.)

The reason I am highlighting this is not because I think you should race to your chosen school on the day of your child's birth and get them enrolled (although I actually had to do this for one family I worked for, and the child turned out to be the last one to be enrolled for that year), it's to remind you that you do need to do a wee bit of forward planning. Babies are being born every day and we can't ignore the fact that there simply aren't enough preschools or childminders to accommodate them in their early years. I have found this to be the case all over. So, this is what I advise you to think about when you have a wee one.

Firstly, are you planning on going back to work? If yes, then who is going to be looking after your most precious creation? Family? Nanny/childminder? (If so, will they be full-time or part-time?) Daycare/kindergarten/preschool? A bit of everything?

Whatever you decide, maternity leave goes way too quickly, and you need to have your childcare arrangements in place *before* you actually need them. Daycare centres, especially the good ones, are always in demand and usually have waiting lists. So, get on it! Sometimes, you will have to pay a deposit to show your intent, but regardless, try to get your baby's name down as early as you can. It's better to have a place and then not need it than to need a place and not have it.

The same goes for preschools. Even if you are able to look after them yourself until they are of school age, you both may need some breaks/social time. I highly recommend popping them into a preschool for a morning or an afternoon a couple of times a week. This isn't just for the sake of your sanity; it will also get them socialised and provide invaluable preparation for classroom life. Plus, it's fun for them and they'll make great crafts that can be given to grandparents to cherish on a monthly basis. They also cover all the holiday cards – it's win-win on the art front!

You will need to scout out the preschools in your area that work best for you. Also, factor in whether it can be a feeder to your chosen school in later years. Does their method of teaching/learning match what you have in mind? Are there separate classrooms or are all ages in together? Are there open, green spaces nearby that they can use, or do they have access to a playground? Will the staff help with potty training or expect you to cover this? What's the teacher/child ratio and what kind of phonics teaching system do they use? I've seen the latter change many times over. How you were taught isn't how they teach things today, so it's good to get on board with up-to-date thinking. Later on, you'll find this with maths – they do it in a completely different way. The answers might be the same, but I sure can't help my older kids with their homework anymore.

You do need to either get their name down on a waiting list or provide the preschool/nursery with their start date, so it's advisable to find out exactly what the protocol is. My wee one is only 16 months, but I have her down for a place as it comes up, which could be in six months or a year's time. They usually hold annual open days/walkaround visits, so keep an eye out in your local paper and in hotspots such as libraries and town halls, etc. Go and have a nosey. Ask about the place. Chatting to previous inmates, I mean attendees, is always wise. Your local education authority should have health and safety ratings and other information available to the public.

Childminders are always in high demand. Some offer preschool and big school pickups, which means your child can be with the same person for a number of years. As a former nanny, I know that consistency is reassuring to parents. They are all insured and vetted to the highest standard (or should be), so when choosing who will be looking after your wee one, don't be shy about wanting to see all their certificates and policies. They'll happily have it all available for you to view. You are paying, so get what you need and want.

Most of all, educate yourself as to what you want your child to get out of any experience, be that with a childminder or at preschool. There are many, pardon the pun, schools of thought about how best to look after and educate a child during their early years. I know it's a weird one to think about while your wee one is so wee, but gone are the days when you could rock up at a preschool and get them enrolled a week before they are due to start. A mum I recently spoke with was pleased I had given her the heads up, so I thought I would do the same for you.

Play Away

As a nanny in a previous life, I was well aware of the importance of coffee groups and playgroups, as they provided a lifeline to the community. I made it a priority to get the lowdown on local classes and playdates, as well as good playgrounds to help my charges forge friendships. It was also a good opportunity for me to meet other nannies and make my own connections. Now, as a mummy, the exact same priorities apply.

I am glad to say there will be a playgroup/coffee group/ breastfeeding group, etc., going on every day somewhere in your area, and if not, there's always the playground (weather permitting).

And I can't tell you enough, get out of the house and get yourself to one. My wee one and I have been going to one group or another since she was very little, and you need to as well. There will be groups that meet up specifically for your wee one's age, ranging from newborn to threenager, so you don't need to worry about them getting trampled by older kids. You can relax and feed (and cry if needed) with other mums who are going through exactly the same thing as you. Coffee and cakes are always provided (believe me, caffeine, sugary things and company are the Holy Grail), along with toys, mats and comfy couches. You can't go wrong.

As my wee one is now on her feet, she has graduated to an age-appropriate and active playgroup, where she can hone her new skills and learn from others. It's basically rowdier and more rambunctious than the get togethers we had with newborns or crawlers, and she loves it. It has slides and sandpits, cars and trucks and building blocks and ball pits. She has learned to move about the space and be aware of others racing around. She plays away from me and with others, or quietly by herself in her own world. She also knows she has to take turns on equipment or wait until whatever she wants to play with is free. Today, she had to actively get someone else to play with her, as she found a seesaw and raced over to it in the hope another kid would climb on the other side.

These playgroups in the winter and playgrounds in the summer are where mums can congregate, have a coffee and get some adult conversation in. Everyone young and old(er) can perfect their social skills, as meeting new people can be hard when you're out of the workplace. Turning up somewhere new, especially with wee ones in tow, is daunting, but kids also provide an ice breaker. Trust me, sit for five minutes and someone will talk to you with whom you'll find common ground. You might even meet a lifelong friend for both you and your child. Faces will become familiar and greetings will turn from making eye contact to a smile and then to a hug, and that's not just your kids. Invites to playdates and birthday parties will ensue and you'll see your new friends at other classes, soft play centres and in the street. This new community will provide a safety net for you, and you'll receive some all-important reassurance from others who are in the same boat.

As you get to know some fellow parents, your child will learn a new safe place in which to be themselves, and they'll grow in confidence as they watch and learn from others. I swear my wee one mastered crawling and walking from these places. She studied the bigger kids, something clicked in her mind and off she went, quite literally. Going to a place with others of a similar age each week instills a routine for all involved. There's an expectation of fun, so everyone looks forward to the meetings. When you have had a tough time the day, night or weekend before, playgroups/grounds offer a refuge and a break for the weary, as there will be many mums watching the children.

These occasions can also build up your child's courage for later in their early life, as they will learn how to make new friends and be autonomous. This will help prepare them for when they start going to preschool, day care, kindergarten and eventually to school, where, due to play spaces in your local area, they may know a few faces already. It will be a huge relief to both parent and child that these 'first days' aren't so scary and unfamiliar.

I would go as far as to say that playgroups/coffee groups and playgrounds are an essential building block and tool that needs to be utilised. I feel it's essential in shaping a little person into a well-rounded, good natured and sociable child and adult. Churches and community centres often run these types of gatherings really well, and some are even free, requiring perhaps just a small donation to go towards the food. They are usually run by parents themselves and/or retired midwives/health visitors and kind grannies, who can offer you a wealth of childcare knowledge. So, do get out of the house and get yourself and bubs to one of these. I swear you will feel better for rocking up.

Water Baby

Until I got lazy and circumstances stopped us from going to the pool every week, my wee one was a real water baby. When I finally took her swimming again after a month's hiatus, she was afraid of being submerged. It didn't help that she had showered with us rather than being bathed. In fact, she became so terrified of the bath that I had to get in with her. So, this post is about how important it is to get your baby into the water as quickly and as much as you can.

Here are some ways to get you both in the drink:

Get in the bath

Nothing is quite as relaxing as plopping bubs on your chest and having skin-on-skin contact in a warm bath. Pop them in the kitchen or bathroom sink to begin with and then graduate to a baby bath or big bath. They are born of water and it will feel natural to them, bringing peace, familiarity and safety.

Get in a pool

To begin with, swimming lessons for wee ones are expensive (although they're worth investing in for older tots), so find your local leisure centre and scope out safe swim times for parents and babies. Swish them around and get them used to a larger volume of water than the bath. They will not be afraid to float around and be taken under, and they will naturally close their throats to prevent inhaling any water. (This is something young babies can do with ease, as it's reminiscent of being in the womb. It also means they can breathe and breast or bottle feed at the same time. Sadly, they do lose this ability with age.) Bobbing about, learning to splash and kick and play with toys, etc., will give you both confidence. Once they are bigger, any time from six months to a year, enrol them in lessons. There they will learn survival methods: going under, reaching for the side, holding on, kicking, floating and climbing out. Then keep going. Soon, they will be in the pool without you!

When you are at the seaside, walk into the water until you are ankle deep, with your little one in your arms. Waves can be scary, especially the bigger ones. So, hold them in the wash and dip them in and out so they can get used to them. You can even let older tots chase you up and down. If it's warm enough, sit in the shallows and let the waves wash over you. It's good for wee ones to know the sound and taste of the sea. But as it can be dangerous, too, teach them to stay in the shallows and to be mindful. It's all about confidence.

Paddle time

If the weather permits, invest in a paddling pool. Fill her up and invite the neighbours' kids around. On a hot day, they can enjoy hours of supervised fun by hopping in and out. With a past job, I used to blow the pool up with fresh water in the morning, let it heat up in the sun and then dump a whole load of toys in. The wee one would jump in and float around, picking up toys from the bottom. I swear she was part fish and preferred being under water.

Sprinkler

If it's hot enough and they need to cool down, letting wee ones play with water is always fun. Fill a bucket and let them pour water from one cup to another. (This must be supervised, as small children can drown in even a small amount of water. Never, ever leave them alone!) For toddlers who can stand, invest in a water table with slides and shoots. Think marble run with water. Bigger ones love to be brave and run through a moving sprinkler (which will be watering the lawn at the same time). You can get sprinklers that double up as toys and shoot off in all directions. For the even bigger kids, water pistols are great. You can get small ones that don't really get you wet, or, if you're brave enough, super soakers. Water balloons are also lots of fun.

Water parks

Even if you don't live near a giant water attraction with slides and rides, most councils have invested in a water park that everyone can go to for free. They usually comprise fountains that shoot up out of the ground or overhead for kids to sit or run in. I used to pop my wee one in a wetsuit and let her be free. (The wetsuit verses a swimsuit allows her to stay in/under/out for longer, as children get cold easily – even on hot days.)

My husband has taken up kayaking, so when the wee one is older, she will be plopped in the middle with a life jacket on and paddled around. There are so many great options for confident older children, including boating, sailing, paddleboarding and surfing.

What to wear

Being from New Zealand, you can burn in five minutes, so Slip-Slop-Slap is engrained in me and I'm an all coverage girl. (Slip on a neck-to-knee suit or rash vest, slop on some suncream and slap on a hat.) All the kids in my care are guaranteed to be well covered and there are great options for all ages, including all-in-one spf suits for indoor and outdoor use, either one-piece or two-piece. There are also thinner wetsuits and baby wraps for wee ones, so they don't get cold as fast. For toileting, there are swim nappies, both disposable (boo hiss) and reusable (yay). You can buy floats to pop the baby in and armbands and jackets with buoyancy aids that can be removed as your little one becomes more confident. However, I am not an advocate of using them, as I feel it gives babies a false sense of security, etc., and when you teach them how to swim with confidence, they won't need all the other stuff.

For the girls, I invest in a swim cap. Not those rubber ones that you had to squeeze into like a glove, but ones made of soft material that dries quick. Girls tend to have longer hair, which gets in their eyes. No amount of hair ties and clips will stop it plastering their face when they surface. With a cap it's out of the way and fuss free.

I also got my charges into wearing goggles, so they could open their eyes under the water. It helped with their level of enjoyment and meant their eyes didn't become puffy and sore.

I am pleased to say that after my wee one's initial trepidation, she found her fun bone and started splashing and playing again in both the pool and the bath. But I learned a valuable lesson, or more relearned one, that you need to keep up the coverage. She naturally warmed to the pool, as it was familiar when she was little, but as an older baby, she had forgotten it and needed to be reminded how much fun it was. As I said at the beginning, swimming, water confidence, knowing what to do when you fall in, or even just getting water in your eyes or over your head, should be a part of life for most people and taught to our wee ones from day dot. Get into the pool, dance in the waves, pay for lessons and then watch so you can reinforce the instructions later. You will feel happier that your child knows how to handle themselves and have fun in the water.

Happy splashing!

Music, a Universal Language

Music is one of the first languages that babies learn. They know a beat from listening to your heart for nine months. The gurgle of your stomach and the sound of your voice has a rhythm. If you played them music, be it inadvertently when you were listening to something or purposely to your tummy while they were in there, they would have gotten to know the cadence, tempo and timings. So, play to that strength (pun intended).

As I said above, play them music when they are in the womb. I recommend classical for wee ones for two reasons. One, you can always find a classical music station on the radio, so, if you have sleep trained them to a relaxing sonata they will instantly know to calm down, as it's bedtime. Secondly, classical music is scientifically proven to stimulate brain waves and improve learning and language. So, exposing your child all through their life, starting with the day they are born (or beforehand), to classical music can't be a bad thing. It will help with cognitive development.

As babies grow, music becomes a great learning tool and a form of fun and expression for everyone taking part. The repetition and rhythm of songs and nursery rhymes is vital for their understanding of the world, and your singing, no matter what key it's in, will be instantly recognisable to them and bring smiles and laughter. Plus, your movements, as you go through the actions related to the nursery rhyme, will help their coordination and motor skills. Think *Head, Shoulders, Knees and Toes* and the counting that you do with *Baa Baa Black Sheep*. If you are still learning the songs, invest in musical books and toys. My wee one has worn the battery down on her *If You're Happy and You Know It* book, which plays as you read.

When they are big enough and you are ready, please get yourself to a music class. The communal singing, dancing and interaction is a vital part of play. The exposure to sound and the physical touch of the instruments stimulates the senses. Your baby will soon start to recognise tunes and participate, as they learn from watching and listening to what others do. Feeling the beat of the music and the repetition of the notes will become familiar and they will get excited when their jam comes on. Right now, *Wind the Bobbin Up* is my wee one's favourite. She used to love *Row Row Row Your Boat*, but tastes change . . .

Music should be a large part of daily life, too. Have it on in the background, whether that's something you want to listen to or a selection of children's songs. I use my Alexa to verbally request the playlists I've created via Amazon Music. My wee one recognises a good beat, usually in the first four bars, and starts bopping along or twerking her bum and swinging her arms. It is wonderful to see her face light up at a song she really loves, such as *Baby Shark* or the *Teletubbies* theme song. A love and understanding of music are something that you don't teach as such, as it seems to be intrinsic in everyone. My little one and I listen and dance around the room to everything, which these days can vary from African drumming, my teens' choice of rappers, nursery rhymes and Top 40 hits. She will get really into some things, forming her own tastes that are separate from mine. I feel it's important to introduce her to as many forms of music as I can.

This takes me nicely to instruments. I wish I had learned to play one. My sister did, and I think it is a wonderful skill to be able to hear, read and play music. While I won't force my daughter to learn to play something unless she expresses an interest, I will give her all the tools she needs to get involved if that's what she wants, starting with basic instruments and ways for her to make her own music. In class, we clap, stamp and use our voices to form sounds and music. Now she is older, both at class and at home, she gets to play with instruments, including bells, whistles, shakers, a tambourine, piano, xylophone and drums. I achieved this veritable orchestra by scouring secondhand shops and through hand-me-downs from friends. It's wonderful to get a band together and for bubs to get involved in making her own sounds. When she hits that drum and inadvertently plays a beat, she is so proud of herself. Instruments don't have to be expensive or even recognisable. A wooden spoon on an upturned saucepan or bowl is just as good. Rice or beans in a container make a great shaker. My wee one loves the sprinkles jar we ordinarily use for decorating cupcakes. It's small enough for her hand and makes a great noise. Paper towels and toilet rolls (once you are done with them) can make wonderful trumpets, as the sound changes as you shout down them. Once they are older, glasses filled with varying volumes of water can make some lovely and differing sounds when tapped.

I have tried to incorporate music into all parts of my little one's life. I've hummed to her whenever she was upset and gently sung her lullabies. I've gotten her familiar with a song to help her relax and sleep, got down on the floor to enact nursery rhymes and created our own 'dancefloor' to actively get her moving to the beat. I've also taken her to class to get her into peer support groups so she can hear, watch and learn from others, and I've found her things to play with so she can express herself. Throughout the day, I have some sort of sound on so her mind is stimulated. Music is a universal language that can soothe, engage and teach. We can get excited about it or use it to unwind. That makes it an invaluable tool for parents and children to communicate with and through for life. I still listen to the albums my dad played to me when I was young. Music connects us all, and it's never too early to start!

On You Like a Rash

My wee one is ill. It's her first real sickness, and she has a temperature and a rash from her head to her toes. It's one of those illnesses that is affecting her whole body but is also non-specific. She is just off her food and wants to be held all the time. It's probably a virus. She is at so many coffee groups, soft plays and playgroups that picking something up must be somewhat inevitable. It's just one of those things, although I did panic and reached for a glass to roll across her tummy and thus rule out the big M – meningitis. Bubs has had her shots, but I'm still terrified of this infection. (If you are at all worried about what the rash is, the rule of thumb is to roll a glass across the skin where the rash is at its reddest. If it goes white/ disappears under the pressure, then you don't need to worry so much, but if the spots remain red under the glass, then get your child to A&E, as it may be more serious.) My worries eased when I realised it wasn't something potentially life-threatening, and I was able to return to treating her general malaise and the rash.

Thanks to my career as a nanny, I've had to be Florence Nightingale many times over, and I know my rash encyclopedia inside and out, which means I don't make rash assumptions (pun intended!). Instead, I will wait and see. Sometimes, a rash is just a rash. It may be caused by a virus that is making its way through the body, or it can simply be a heat rash. It may develop into pityriasis rosea, which looks bad but doesn't really knock them, or worsen into hand, foot and mouth disease, chicken pox or slapped cheek syndrome, which can all make children feel quite sick. Hopefully, it won't be measles, as most kids these days have had a jab to stop them getting it. There are itchy, scaly or peeling rashes that are reactions to something, such as food, washing powder, pollen, you name it. With so many possible causes, at first, it's best just to keep an eye on things.

But it's hard when they are ill, especially if you haven't experienced it before and your wee one goes from operating at a hundred miles an hour to slow mode overnight. They'll be blotchy and grumpy and want to be held and then put down again ten seconds later. They can't tell you how they feel, they just feel horrible and want you to make it go away. They will be hungry but not eat, tired but unable to sleep. Here is what to do.

Cancel all your plans. You now have a date with the TV remote, be it to watch their programmes or yours. They won't feel like doing anything. It's best to keep them away from others, from a day to a week or so, depending on what they have.

Look online and try and identify the rash from reputable websites. Contact your doctor if you need further help with identifying it, or for advice on care.

Have plenty of fluids on hand, as they won't eat. Don't panic about this. That lovely round tummy they have is for this exact moment. It's a store of fats to live off when they feel bad. Once they are well again, they will restock it by eating you out of house and home . . .

Sleep, sleep, sleep. Let them snooze for however long they want to, as it's a wonderful way for their bodies to recoup. Don't wake a sleeping baby, even if they go over their rest times. Sometimes, you will have a bad night when they are feeling off, so take the opportunity to rest, too. Mind you, they may just want to sleep on you, so you won't have any other choice but to be still!

Get out the snacks. They won't eat at mealtimes, so don't bother with them, but do give them the opportunity to nibble throughout the day if they want to. This will boost their blood sugar levels. I put out a plate full of soft foods, such as cut-up fruits, muesli bars and strips of toast, etc. I keep it close by and encourage them to pick at it.

Warm baths. Use oats and hypoallergenic soaps so as not to irritate the rash.

Let them lie on you in comfy, non-scratch clothes, and with whatever comfort items they require, be it a dummy firmly placed in their mouth all day, or their teddy bear to cling onto. Or go old school and return to skin-on-skin. This helps to regulate their temperature/digestive system. Strip off from the waist up (both you and baby) before snuggling together under a blanket. Your skin, smell and chest/neck are their first ever safe spaces and comfort zones.

Get comfy yourself. Just like when you were feeding them during those first few weeks and months, have all you need to hand, too, including drinks, phone, the remote, etc.

The best medicine for your wee one is you. If you're relaxed and calm and not panicky then they will be, too, and you can snuggle in and have a few duvet days together, recouping and resting. They will be back to fighting fit in no time, and you'll miss the quiet. But of course, if you are at all worried about them, see a health care professional, either a doctor or pharmacist (pharmacists are an untapped resource and usually very helpful), or go to A&E, if you feel you need to. Your wee one is your Number One priority.

I can't say I hope you never go through the sick baby phase, because you will, so once you have reassured yourself it's not something serious (and even I do this every time), you can be everything they need to help them through it safely and quickly. Now, I'm going back to the couch for an afternoon snuggle.

Baby Jail

I know I may be preaching to the converted and that some of you will say, 'I have been doing that for months', but hopefully others will declare, 'Why didn't I think of that?' and my words won't have been wasted. I am talking here about travel cots being used as playpens, AKA Baby Jail. I have used this tactic in past jobs when houses were multi-level and I needed to keep wee ones and siblings from going up and down the stairs. Stair gates were in place, but at one house the older child, who was four, couldn't figure them out and, therefore, was never good at shutting them. Hence, I needed a way of keeping little people contained while I did a job for which I needed neither company nor help.

Travel cots are easy to erect and store when they're not in use, which means they are a must-have item for any family. They're obviously brilliant for travelling, especially as airlines give them free passage as part of the baby's ticket, and they're also great as a second sleeper/daybed for daytime naps. But when they're not being used for any of that, throw some toys inside and use them whenever you need to pop bubs down and have five minutes to do something important, which could be visiting the loo alone, making dinner or finishing off the last sentence of a blog before the wee one decides she wants to help.

I suggest investing in one from the get-go, either new or second-hand. Alternatively, beg, steal or borrow one. It doesn't have to be flashy – mine has a tiny hole in one side – just make sure you get one with a padded mattress for comfort. Fitted cot sheets wrap nicely over the base. For newborns, you can hang mobiles from the sides and for the crawlers, putting some stuffed animals and books inside should be enough to keep them engaged for the five minutes you need. In containing them inside something with sides, you can leave them for a few minutes knowing they will be safe and secure. I especially recommend them for when you have two-plus kids in your charge. One can be in a bouncer, with the other in Baby Jail. You can then get a few things done knowing they are strapped and trapped. When the aforementioned kids I looked after as a nanny were old enough to play together but still too young to be left to their own devices, this was a great method for getting them to interact. Although we had the cot for the younger sibling to go in, one day I found the older one in there. When I asked why he'd chosen that particular spot, he replied, 'It's the only place she can't get me!'

There are a few other options available on the market, such as a gated playpen, which you can use to keep the wee one in place, but

I find that the travel cot works just as well for this purpose, as well as for what it's designed for. So, when you buy one, it's really a two-for-one deal.

For anyone who may not have considered this option, I suggest you either go out and buy a travel cot, or dust off the one you may already have, shove some toys in for the wee one to play with and enjoy five minutes to yourself with a cup of tea. After all, it's good for babies to learn to play by themselves. I keep my travel cot close to hand at all times. It's stocked and ready to be dragged around the house as required. My wee one loves it so much she even asks to get in it. I'm encouraging her, as I know it won't be long before she can get out of jail all by herself.

Flying with Precious Cargo

So, I did a thirty-three-hour, door-to-door trip to New Zealand with my four-month-old, and it was great. After nannying for so many years, I knew exactly what I was in for and what to pack. Of course, as she was so young, she slept the whole time, could be laid flat and didn't need toys or entertaining. Four months later, I took her on a one-hour flight from Belfast to London and quickly realised I had to up my game. The plane was delayed by an hour and a half, which would have been fine except for the fact it was an eight pm flight. Bubs soon became overtired and she was a wriggle bum, threw stuff around, annoyed our fellow passengers, kicked the back of the seat, cried, yelled and needed food to be constantly stuffed in her face. Yes, travelling with kids is fraught with disasters waiting to happen. My sister did the same trip to New Zealand with three kids in tow. One came down with a tummy bug mid-flight and vomited everywhere, before pooping so much they ran out of nappies. I use this example as a worst-case scenario. With a wee bit of crisis planning and a disaster kit (as in pack the right things), you can enjoy a less stressful journey.

When travelling with children, it quickly comes to light just how much you need to take with you. However, try not to fall into the trap of panicking and over packing. Many problem scenarios are similar and can be covered with the same basics.

Here are a few things I learnt as a nanny, which I now practise as a parent.

Timing is everything

If it's a long flight, book a night one so you at least have the hope they will sleep through it. For flights over two or three hours, and if you can afford it, book them a seat to themselves, even if they are under two. This is a pricier option, but it will give you and them space, which is invaluable in the long run.

If you're planning a short-haul flight, try to book one that doesn't overlap with their usual naptimes, as if they can't get comfy, they will yell. Even though you shouldn't feel responsible, you will feel like every pair of eyes on the plane is tracked on you.

Hand luggage

The rule of thumb is to only take the essentials that will cover you for the duration of your journey (that includes car time).

Food. If the journey crosses over with a snack or mealtime, take it with you, then discard any leftovers and wash out the milk bottle, as it can be used again and again (airport staff and flight attendants will be happy to steam clean a bottle or plate/bowl for you). Alternatively, you could also buy a bottle of water to drink and then use the bottle for milk. I carry the powder for formula in a small divider that holds three measured portions. You can buy these from most pharmacies, and they are a godsend for travelling.

Double up. Take two of whatever they need to relax/sleep. For my wee one, that means packing two dummies and two muslins. I do this because it's sod's law that one will get lost at the bottom of the bag at exactly the wrong moment.

Warm up. Take a blanket with you, as it'll get cold on the aeroplane.

Good coverage. When it comes to nappies, as a rule of thumb, I pack five to cover a twenty-four-hour period. This is also when I allow myself to use disposables. Reusables are too hard to take with you on a flight; who wants to carry around soiled nappies? I also take a full pack of wipes, nappy sacks and cream.

Playtime. I pack very few toys, perhaps a couple of their favourites, but never ones that contain small parts or are battery operated. (You don't want the embarrassment of something going off at the wrong moment!). Keep in mind that they will probably just want to play with whatever is in the seat pocket anyway.

First Aid. I pack Calpol (the individual sachets), teething powder (this is also great for calming bigger babies) and Vaseline, as their lips will get very dry.

Wear it well. Take clothes that are multi-use, such as babygrow pjs that they can sleep or play in. It's also just one thing to change, rather than having to fiddle around with multiple tops and bottoms. Take at least two.

Snack time. Pack them a small container of their favourite foods. If they're on solids, this could be some raisins, crackers and pre-cut fruit, etc. You could also give them a sippy non-spill cup full of juice. The act of chewing and/or sucking from a cup or bottle will also distract them and help their ears to pop during takeoff and landing, alleviating any discomfort.

Distraction techniques. For older kids who have the attention span to watch something, forget all the talk about restricting tech and load up a tablet with their favourite telly programmes. Make sure it's fully charged and pack headphones to minimise the noise for your fellow passengers.

Checked baggage

I've found that airlines, in general, are really good at helping parents with young ones in tow, so it's a good idea to do some research before you travel and find out what's available. If bubs is going to be on your lap, you may be charged a higher fee but will be afforded some perks, including boarding early. Some airlines allow you to check in two baby/toddler items for free (outside of your checked baggage), including a car seat and a buggy.

Seating arrangements. Try to secure a seat towards the back of the plane, as it will be closer to the loos and you will be using them more. However, if you're too close to the galley, the bustling and banging of the aircrew may wake bubs, unless, of course, you are right at the front with a bassinet – happy days!

Double up. Take clothing that can be worn twice or more and be mixed and matched, such as cardigans and jumpers that go with everything and tights that can be worn under several outfits, etc. Take a weather-appropriate hat, and if it's going to be cold, pack a thick jacket. Be practical.

Hours of fun. Pack a few choice toys, the type that keep on giving, such as stacking cups and shape sorters. For older kids, puzzles are great, as they can do them again and again (to save space, take them out of the box and put them into a cloth bag). Crayons and colouring/sticker books are similarly entertaining.

Bathtime. Don't worry about packing towels, flannels and bath toys, your accommodation should provide the former and the stacking cups can be used to keep them occupied in the bath.

Mealtimes. Take one or two bowls that come with cutlery that either fits inside them or clips to the top.

Remember that when you need some extra space or you find your suitcase is too heavy, it is easy to pare down your baby stuff. Most little ones will be happy simply to be on holiday and you will find other ways to entertain them, without taking the kitchen sink. This may even make you realise that you have rather overindulged bubs at home by thinking they won't be able to function without this or that. They can and will, so it's a bit of a reality check.

Travelling with a baby or a small child doesn't have to be daunting, I promise (and I have been doing it for twenty-five years). But you do have to plan ahead, get your timings right and pack the right stuff.

Safe journey. x

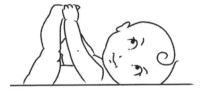

Do Not Disturb

My daughter is becoming more independent, spending more time in her own head. She's figuring things out and lightbulb moments are popping up all the time. You can see it in her eyes as she pieces together parts of her world. She's trying to convey this with speech; chatting up a storm, interjecting in conversations and calling out to people – not in English, but she thinks she is! She is problem solving and experimenting and, most importantly, playing. Yes, they all play, I hear you say, and yes, that's true, but it's the type of play they exhibit that is so wonderful and so important.

Our babies/toddlers learn pretty much everything through play. They learn to eat through very messy play at the table or while sitting in their highchair. Through trial and error during play, they learn to do things like shape sorting and stacking. They also grasp how to take turns and interact with others in a social environment. And the most important play of all, which only comes with time and opportunity, which we need to encourage and foster, is *imagination* play.

My daughter has started to use her 'language' and her imagination in play. She acts things out with toys, especially soft toys or ones that are recognisable as having a function, such as cars, tools and dolls, etc. She's started to make up wee scenarios in her head, and I will often find her talking to her toys. She is very loving towards them, and each one gets a cuddle. It is very sweet.

For two reasons, these wee connections she is forming were very prevalent during our holiday a few weeks ago. Firstly, she was able to entertain herself. The sand on the beach we were on was very hot, so poor bubs was held hostage by the beach blanket and umbrella shade provided. But she made the most of it by collecting rocks and stacking them. As she collected different sizes of stones and rocks, she changed the way she played with them. The most interesting change was her voice. She spoke normally to the big ones and in a higher pitch to the smaller ones, just like we do with babies. It was wonderful to watch, which brings me to my second observation, which is that in these situations we must only observe. And this can be hard to do.

We sometimes feel that we need to entertain our kids and/or get involved with them if they look like they are not 'doing' anything. But I disagree. I feel that if they are happy bumbling around in their own heads then leave them be.

I find there is always someone who thinks doing 'nothing' is literally wasteful, but that misses the point. My husband is not good at this, and if he sees her doing 'nothing' he will start messing around with her. My wee one will be happy in her head, but he will come over and tickle her or try to instigate a different game. She (and I) then get annoyed and he doesn't know why. I'm trying to convince him to save his diversions, distractions and interactions for when she is actively looking for something to do. He finds it hard to read the signals that she is happy to do her own thing. As we know, kids will attach themselves to you. Whether you're going to the bathroom, bedroom or having a sit down, they will gravitate to where you are. So, when bubs is happy and lost in a game of their own making, try to step back and let them be. They will always find you!

I had a dad once, back when I was a nanny, who, as soon as I had his kids settled and playing with things, would come in, clap his hands and say, "They're not doing anything, what activity have you got planned?" I don't know if it was just because he wanted his money's worth out of me, or whether it was that he simply didn't understand that kids playing with their imagination is invaluable in later life for self-confidence and being happy in their own company, which leads to self-starting. I gently told the dad that I was teaching his kids not to hang around his ankles at weekends looking for him to supply entertainment and provide constant stimulation. I'm happy to say he learned my life lesson and let me get on with it.

Imagination is a wonderful tool in which children problem solve, figure things out, make sense of things and entertain themselves. Trust me, it becomes invaluable when they are older and aren't always at your feet, whining, "I'm bored!" Imagination also leads to daydreaming, which is one of the tools for coping and stress management. How much would you love a minute to yourself right now? Yet we interrupt our kids just when they are cognitively working things out . . .

This also goes for pootling, pottering and wandering, etc. As J. R. R. Tolkien said, "Not all those who wander are lost." This is very true for toddlers and kids. They like to just wander around, take in the space and observe. It's wonderful when they are young if you can give them a safe space to just toddle about in. I call my daughter's space 'the rat run'. I have created a circuit through the kitchen, hallway, lounge, playroom and spare room that leads to the garden (all interconnected with doors). It is toddler proofed and she can play wherever and with whatever takes her fancy. This usually entails rearranging my bookcase and dropping off toys and items from the playroom in weird and wonderful spots. The ball pit is systematically emptied and redistributed around the aforementioned rooms. I will always be present in one of the rooms, and she acknowledges me as she goes by, but I mainly leave her to it and collect up the trail of destruction at the end of the day. She is often happy to pootle about, lost in her own agenda and being very independent. When the weather is nice and she is older, I'll open the door to the garden and let her be free and feral in a natural space. There is so much to be learned from exploring your environment, both inside and out, and this can be both very calming and stimulating for your child. There is fun to be had in all kinds of weather; from making mud pies and daisy chains to playing ball games and creating huts with all the kitchen chairs. Imagination play is the best.

So, if you find you come in to see your child lost in a game, an activity that is engaging them so much that they don't even know you are there, stop, back out of the room, go and make a cuppa and enjoy a moment to yourself. Whatever you do, DO NOT DISTURB.

In the Blink of an Eye

I looked away for a second, as I helped another mother with her wee woman, and she was gone. She had been bustled out of the door by a group of chatting mums who, not really paying attention, had absorbed her into their gaggle. It was the Halloween party of our music class, and it was being held at a community centre. All the kids were dressed the same, in black outfits, etc. They were also around the same age, so this was easily done. Ten seconds later, I found her wandering around the entrance looking as happy as anything. My mother's instinct had kicked in and I had done a quick look around the hall, ascertained she wasn't there and shoved my way out of the exit. Luckily, she hadn't strayed far, and there was a caretaker on hand at the outer door for this exact reason. It was a push button exit, which even us adults find hard to use and often curse, well, not anymore. I will never fuss about having to hit that button and then manhandle the kids out of the door. I have never been so thankful for that tricky exit.

My heart was racing, and I felt as though it was also missing some beats. There was panic in my voice, as adrenaline rushed around my body. The separation lasted no more than a few seconds, but this frantic feeling hit me hard, as this was the first time I'd lost *her*. As a nanny, I know this kind of thing happens all the time. They are usually just around the corner or out of sight for a split second. And although this was the first time, I know it won't be the last. Whether you're at a playground, supermarket or coffee morning, they can wander off, and we have to be vigilant at all times. Mistakes can be made, of course, but I would not wish a lost child on anyone. It's a parent's worst nightmare. After they have been located and hugged so much they can barely breathe, these tales of lost children can make for funny stories, but we'll also never forget the sheer relief we felt when we got them back.

My best lost child story involves my sister. As a toddler, she wandered off in an airport bookshop of all places. As my parents and I frantically scrambled around the place looking for her, she got herself handed in to lost and found. She was in there for a while and in all her wisdom decided to change her name. When asked, she denied her real identity, meaning we nearly missed our plane. We laugh now, but back then I think my parents wanted to kill her as much as kiss her. Years later, my sister lost her son while on holiday in Italy, when he ran off in a crowd. So, no matter what your history or your parenting skills and experience, at some point your kid will get lost.

This leads me nicely onto highlighting a steep learning curve and a duality when it comes to parenting. On the one hand, we need to watch them constantly; they are fast and curious and don't know the ways and the dangers of the world. On the other hand, the world needs to be explored and they need to learn to be independent of us. This is hard. I guess they need to know they are safe at a certain distance, but that they should not stray too far. I would not wish losing a child, even for a second, on my worst enemy, but a dose of panic is good for all of us, otherwise we may become too complacent, and that is when the worst can happen.

When you do lose them, and it will happen in varying degrees over the years, and then get them back (eventually), you will feel like you have failed. But you need to understand this happens to everyone, no matter what or where or how. If/when you lose them, even for a second, yell out, ask for help, get everyone involved. The sooner you do this, the sooner you'll find them. And it will remind everyone else to be careful with their own children. When your child is found, everyone will feel a sense of collective relief. We need to remember as parents to take care and be responsible for others. Look out for the kids who aren't yours, listen out for wee ones calling for help. I have lost count of the times I have reunited a child with their panic-stricken parents. We're all in this together.

I hope you never know that feeling of fear you get when you don't know exactly where your child is, so here are some tips to minimise the risk.

Communicate with your partner when you're together. Who has got him/her? Make eye contact with them and ensure they know that they are in charge now. I have witnessed a wee one wander off unnoticed in a busy food hall, as each parent thought the other had her. I scooped her up and returned her to her embarrassed dad, who was being yelled at by her distraught mum. Obviously, communication with the child is key, too. Tell them to keep hold of your hand and not to wander off.

Don't Panic. Rather than running around, stay put and scan the area. Although it's hard, keep calm and slowly take in the details of the area you're in, and where your child may have gone.

Call out. Sometimes, they are just behind you and will reappear at the sound of your voice. Also, other mums, dads and passers-by will pick up on what's going on and will help look for your child, too.

Get organised. When they are wee, strap them into something, be it a shopping trolley or a pushchair, etc. When they are contained, you can do whatever you need to do safe in the knowledge that you can take your eye off them for a split second. If immobilising them to make sure they stay put isn't an option and you are somewhere safe-ish (i.e. not in a car park, etc.), get them to sit down next to you. If they get up, you will notice their movement and quickly be able to grab them. I've found that if they're standing by you, they're able to slip into ninja mode. A good tactic to employ right from the get-go is to train your brain to tick them off first as safe, before moving onto the things that can become distracting and consuming. They'll be off as you answer your phone or go to pick up something, so before you let your concentration drift elsewhere, make sure first that they are safe within your sight.

Hold onto a piece of their clothing, etc. My wee one is at that age where she is walking and standing upright but won't hold my hand for long. I find that during times when I can't give her my full attention, just keeping a hand on her sleeve or hood reassures me she's keeping with me.

Rein them in. If they have a tendency to run off in the opposite direction, there is no harm in using a child harness. At times, my wee one is just shy of understanding and obeying instructions. I don't have the strength to hold her in my arms, as she wriggles and tries to get away. So, at these times, she gets a backpack with a harness inside to keep her with me while still feeling independent.

Even though my wee one is still young, I have started introducing her to some of my safety rules, which I'll do more of when she's old enough to really comprehend them.

My big ones are:

Hand on car. When we are getting in and out of the vehicle, she has to put her hand on the car until I am ready to assist her. This is very handy when you have more than one kid in your charge. Even at her tender age, my little one is getting the hang of this.

Hand on pushchair. When she wants to walk independently, she has to stay within a safe distance of the pushchair. We have a strap that she can hold onto in crowded places.

To the corner only. When she starts to ride a balance bike or scooter, I have a rule that she must only go to the end of the street and then stop. She must also never cross the street without an adult.

Where I can see you. When we start frequenting playgrounds and larger spaces, I will be telling her to stay where I can see her. She will also see me checking that she's following this instruction.

From my years of looking after kids for a living, I know that it is only a matter of time before I misplace my daughter for another second or so – it is simply bound to happen. But the feeling is the same no matter whose child it is in your care. And that feeling stays with you for days, along with the shame, blame (of yourself) and guilt. To try and avoid this trauma, just try your absolute hardest to be aware of where your wee one is at all times, and keep a close eye on everyone else's children, too. Lesson relearned.

THE MOTHERLOAD
(BLOGS FOR MUMMY)

Mary Poppins vs Mother Nature

Twice in two days, I have been asked the same question: "Is being a mum different from being a nanny?" The easy answer is yes – one is paid, you clock off and get to hand them back (eventually). When I was pregnant, I hated it when other parents said, "You won't know what's hit you when the baby comes." Of course, I knew the bond would be different, but with twenty-five years' experience in childcare, I figured that the technique and application would be the same. And it transpired that I was right not to listen to those naysayers. At the same time, there were differences that I wasn't expecting, so just for you, I have compiled my top five.

1. **Just how much you love your kid**. I mean, I can't get enough of bubs. We sit and stare at each other, we play together and we are each other's world. When she is sleeping, I miss her. I loved my charges, I really did. I am still in contact with most of them. We played and hung out, but the connection to your own child, that invisible maternal umbilical cord, produces a love I have never known before. It is complete, unconditional and full of trust on both sides. It is all encompassing and so deep that it takes my breath away.

2. **I can't do it on my own**. As a nanny, I was doing it on my own, all day, for five days a week. I was in charge of all aspects of the lives of the kids in my care, from getting them up, dressed, fed and out of the door, to what they did in the outside world. I drew with them, did puzzles, dressed up, danced around and played with cars, dolls or Lego. I was a professional and this was the job. Now I can't imagine doing all this without the knowledge that help is available from friends and family. Hats off to the single parents, I bow down to you, I really do! You are super mums (and dads). I get through my day by having a 'thing' for me, be it a food shop or a class, as I crave human conversation and

connection. This leads me to the most unexpected part of parenting . . .

3. **How inefficient I am now.** Like I've said, before it was a job (though I hate to put small people in that box), and I was a professional and had to adhere to certain conditions from the parents who employed me. Obviously, my first priority was to keep the children safe. But I was being paid to cover the basics, as well as some extras. I did the shopping, the laundry, the tidying and all the cooking. I also got involved in playdates and classes, did the school runs and took cars in for their MOT. These days, I have trouble scheduling a shower! My wee one and I just kind of float along and I feel like I get nothing done. It is getting better now she is older, as she can sit and entertain herself while I hang out some clothes or do some cooking. But the funny thing about this is that I don't care about my inefficiency. When I was employed, I used to stress myself out if I didn't get everything on my list done, but now if we have a duvet day, I tell myself it's OK. It is weird how your priorities change. Some have shifted, but others have literally disappeared, as if in a puff of smoke.

4. **Not enough hours in the day.** My days at work used to drag a bit. I guess it was because I was doing a job and had a life outside of it that I was raring to get on with. But now there are not enough hours in the day, and I don't mean to just get stuff done (see above), but to actually be with my daughter. I thought being a new mum would be comparable to the jobs I had where I looked after really young babies. I thought I would just feel a wee bit more love for my own child than I did for the kids I helped to raise. After all, being a nanny is a full-on job and you get very attached. But now time just flows by so fast. Before I know it, it's lunch then dinner then bedtime, and another day has passed . . . then another week. The nine months gestation period felt like so

long, especially towards the end (you hear me, sister), but my wee one is almost seven months, so she's been out almost as long as she was in. Where did that time go? Well, it certainly went with joy, the joy of just relishing every little noise and smile. Everything is new and wonderful. I put a veil between me and my charges on purpose, as their firsts were not mine and were for their parents to enjoy. But now, the first times are all mine. That's why I am so possessive of them, I guess. Finally, I get to claim them. And I don't want to miss a thing. If only I could add a few hours to the day . . .

5. **The anxiety.** The physicality of having a baby was new to me. The hormones, too, were bloody hell. I carried her in my body, I birthed her, I nourished her from my body, and I cared for her every hour of every day. This was all a novelty, as was the worry, the ups and downs and the trials and tribulations. In my job, I worked day to day and week to week, not every hour. I did not wake in the night just to check they were breathing or worry about every car journey ending in a head-on collision. Nor did I fret about how the destruction of the planet would affect their future. As you can see, I did suffer with postnatal anxiety. It's a thing and not really talked about, but 'irrational worry', which is different from depression, can be crippling for a new parent. Can I wrap my baby up in cotton wool forever, please?

But the upside to having been a nanny for so long and in all raising about six kids to a good age (and having a hand in raising about sixty others) is that I do know what to expect, good and bad. I know that kids get temperatures and bump their heads and eat dirt sometimes. I know how to feed them solids without worrying what they are eating. I can handle a tantrum and I don't care what others think of me in the shop. I have done over twenty first-aid courses and twenty years of swimming lessons, baby massage classes and music and movement workshops. I could probably run them all single-handedly.

I think the difference between being a nanny and being a mother is that in my past life, the practical gave me confidence and now I have the opportunity to rediscover all the knowledge I gained over those years. I loved being a nanny, but now I see that it was all a pre-run for the best job in the world, which is being my daughter's mum.

Village People

As the old saying goes, it takes a village to raise a child. I always assumed this meant that lots of people – be they family, friends or other mothers/parents – and Joe Blogs are looking out for you and your kids in general. But I recently saw an online discussion between mums, where they talked of missing what their mothers had, where everyone in your street was pretty much at the same stage in life and raising the resident kids together, with grandparents also part of the picture on a daily basis. I understand this, as my friends in New Zealand have this now, whereas I do not. My friends Down Under all had kids around the same time, so their little ones attend the same schools and clubs and they have playdates at each other's houses most days, with the mums taking it in turns to feed the feral gang that has become an extended family. My sister has our parents (and her husband's) on speed dial, and they provide an instant babysitting and taxi service when she can't quite get her kids' schedules to mesh. They live close by and stay over/late a few times a week. In addition, the kids have keys to Granny's house and use it as a second base whenever they need to.

In general, our generation tends to not only move away from their hometown, but they often completely change city and sometimes country, too. This is me. I was pregnant when I moved from London to Northern Ireland, and before that I moved to the UK from New Zealand.

In Ireland, I didn't know anyone, and I mean anyone (except the dad, of course). It's still the case that I have no family here apart from the one I made. This can be quite lonely and isolating at times. When overseas family do come to visit, it's often just for a week here or there. They fit you into a six-part holiday to this half of the world and want to do touristy things rather than just hang out with you, as they would if you were local. You miss out on everyday conversations, birthdays, Christmases and BBQs, as well as memorable moments such as a cousin winning a prize at school or being in a play. I am not complaining, as I have chosen this path, but I do analyse the situation that myself and others have found themselves in as a result of our globetrotting generation.

What I have found is that you must create your own village and not get hung up on what you thought life would be like. In the discussion I mentioned on the previous page, mums lamented the loss of a locational village, but they have found company and support through online groups and the paid for and free groups they've attended. And I can't recommend that enough. It doesn't matter where you find your village, just find one. The tribes of yesteryear are gone, and we are now a mobile lot (in many senses of the word), so we need to find new communities to be part of and even form.

I have a degree in anthropology, and one of the things I noticed in my studies was that the societies we used to be part of and adhere to the values of are a thing of the past. People move around a lot more for work or opportunities. People marry outside their own country and move to be with their spouse, or they make a home with their partner completely separate from where they were each born. People have interests and ideas that lead them to make different life choices from what they expected or was instilled in them. And they find others in this common ground. The wonderful thing is that we form mobs, packs and groups of our own, which overlap and crisscross all facets of our lives. I am part of an infant music group, and I have formed bonds with some of the other members through playdates and coffee mornings outside the class. Likewise, I only see other members of the group in the actual classroom. This is the same in all the other group activities I attend with bubs, including swimming classes and library sessions. I have people I nod to in the street and those I cry down the phone to (because they are in NZ!). I talk regularly online with women I have never met in person and may gossip with others on an hourly basis, even when I have already seen them that day! Just as mothers come in all shapes and sizes physically, so do our social interactions. Just because we might not be lucky enough to share a school run or be able to throw them over Grandpa's fence to play doesn't make our relationships with other people/parents any less valid or meaningful.

But you are going to have to be brave. Unless you're two years old, meeting new people is daunting. It takes guts to open yourself up to new people, even if you do have a common element to break the ice. But you need to step out of your comfort zone, as leading by example is part and parcel of parenting. So, be confident, caring, kind and courageous. Put your anxieties away, take a deep breath and smile. You'll find that both you and your child will benefit. I promise that you *will* meet parents with whom you will click and find a common thread, be that child-related or something from your 'old' life; hopefully, both. I spoke up at an antenatal class and made nine close friends as a result.

And I need my ladies . . . they keep me sane (loosely, we happily admit we are a bit insane), listen, offer advice, ask advice and need me as much as I need them. So, whether your village is virtual, physical, emotional, spiritual or mental (in every way), it is still a lifeline and a support system, and its importance should never be underestimated. Connections are connections, fleeting or deep. So, get out there, make some friends and build a village, brick by brick. Eventually, you'll need a map and a compass just to find your way around it.

By the way, reading this is your first brick, meaning I would be happy to help you build your village. Get in touch. x

Cloth Bum Mum

I am giving myself a pat on the back. I have been ranting about helping to save the planet for years, and now I have a child to pass it onto. Not that I wasn't doing my best before. I was recycling, and I even got the last family I worked for to follow my example. My wee charge used to help me put all the plastic bottles in the right bin, and she even reprimanded her mum when she saw her getting it wrong. Fingers crossed they are still making the effort to recycle now that I'm no longer with them. Back then, I had also started to carry my own reusable bottle and coffee cup. I also turned down straws. (It's a biggy that one. Do you know how many straws are used and thrown away in a day, only to end up in the ocean and up the noses of turtles? Look it up on YouTube, it will change the way you take your drinks forever!) Of course, I had been doing paper and plastics, tins and glass, etc. I even had a food waste box.

But I digress. I got carried away with my own recycling effort there, but as I have said before to anyone who'll listen, for us parents, the biggest way we can do our bit for the planet is via nappies. I'm guessing this issue affects everyone reading this, so I won't hold back. By using disposables, we have done and are doing damage to our planet. Think of them as the devil. They may be easy to use, absorbent, clean and efficient (I sound like one of their ads now), and they do whip moisture away from a baby's skin, but it's plastic that stops that same moisture from getting out. The manufacturers may have improved the absorbent layer inside the nappy, which dissolves into water when it's thrown away, but that outer layer does not. It sits in landfill clogging up Mother Earth's arteries for way too long.

Us mums need to change our outlook, as well as the way we change our babies. We need to stop reaching for the disposables and return to the cloth bum era. For the most part, we grew up wearing them. You know, the old-style ones that were made from terry cloth and folded into all sorts of shapes until we resembled mini sumo wrestlers? Heck, when I was training to be a nanny twenty-five years ago, my first exam was on how to fold and put a cloth nappy on a baby. I am a baby terry cloth and pin origami master. We had to learn how to steep them (which involved popping them into a designated poo bucket to soak out the stains), clean them, fold them and avoid putting extra holes in our babies with the pins. Though trickier (at least back then), cloth nappies have stood the test of time; meanwhile, disposables are part of the plastic generation, a fad if you will, and one that has been proven to have failed. We seem to be afraid to change back, due to misinformation, miscommunication and bloody good marketing. But it's cloth nappies that are the norm. They have been around for far longer than those deceptive disposables. We had a go at the alternative, but now we need to return to what is best for baby, the environment and us parents.

I am pleased to say that my skills as a nappy master are no longer required, as things have moved along. Gone are the pins and plastic outer knickers that badly chafed. Gone are the days of folding, steeping and removing stains. The newfangled terry nappies pretty much self-clean, and there are all-in-one options that go from birth to potty. Velcro has replaced the dreaded pin, and bamboo inners and outers have taken over from plastics. They also wash so well that they can be sold on when your baby is out of nappies. As for the dreaded washing, pop them into the machine at 60 degrees to kill all the nasties and they will dry either outside on the line in the sun and/or on the radiator, which during an Irish winter is inevitably always on. They are slimline, super absorbent (I have found I change my baby less than when I had disposables) and most of all, they are affordable and better for the environment. I recently figured out that my former bosses used to spend more than £5,000 a year on nappies, and over the course of my career, I put over 25,000 of them into landfill.

I've spent £200 on nappies that will last me for the next two years, and many more years after that in a new home. I'm not using the washing machine any more than before, and I'm drying the nappies on a radiator that would have been on anyway. I've also gone the whole way and got my wee one a swim nappy. As we swim every week, this is yet another saving of money and the planet. We have to be responsible in our choices, and we now have some really good options. A growing number of reputable cloth nappy companies offer complete 'systems', etc., so you have no excuse not to give it a try. As well as this blog, there is so much out there to help mothers get on the ladder. Get online and you'll find cloth bum forums, cloth bum support groups and cloth bum resale pages. But look around your area, too. There will be other mums and dads who have joined the revolution, I promise.

I hope that I have persuaded you to at least look into cloth nappies, and perhaps even give them a go. There may be a cloth nappy library in your area, so you can borrow some and try before you buy. In my antenatal group, we have gotten six out of nine babies into a cloth nappy, and we are working on the rest. Trust me, your baby will thank you for the sheer comfort (they too whisk away moisture), and for taking care of the planet they are inheriting from you. I want to thank you for doing your bit, too. Cheers!

Popping Pills

I received some sound advice today from my nail technician. She is also a mum and noticed that my nails were weaker than usual. Apparently, this happens six months after having a baby, in addition to your hair losing the lustre it gained during pregnancy. You may also notice some extra strands coming out on your brush or when you shower. My lovely beauty therapist advised me to take some natural supplements to help combat both of these issues and restore the balance in my body. It got me thinking about two things. One, why aren't new mums warned about this? It's seems just one more thing to add to the list of stuff that happens to us once we have given birth, coming just below letting go of any ambitions we may have harboured to become a professional trampolinist (think bladder). The other thing I contemplated is how making a human from our bodies strips it of all kinds of nutrients, minerals and vitamins. We give our little one everything, not just mentally and emotionally, but physically, too.

Think back to when you were trying to get pregnant or first found out you were expecting. There was a sudden rush to the local health food store or pharmacy to stock up on multivitamins and supplements, perhaps some folic acid, oestrogen, progesterone, royal honey and pineapple (this is what I had to take to get my body ready). There is big business in pregnancy tablets, and lots of brands that sell you this and that for the development of skin, brains, eyes, spinal cords and everything in between. And that's just for the baby! Then, once you are into the trimesters, you may find yourself taking Vitamin D, pills for bone strength, anti-nausea tablets, aspirin, echinacea, probiotics and, in my case, antibiotics. And I am sure some of you took lots of other weird and wonderful stuff. I resembled the counter of a pharmacy, or a pill pusher. (Picture me in an overcoat at baby bump classes, whispering, 'What do you need? I got it all . . . fizzy Love Hearts for heartburn, aspirin for blood thinning.') On a side note, Love Hearts work a treat for heartburn and indigestion, so thank you to whoever gave me that tip!

Then you have bubs and you think it's over . . . it's not.

You still need to work through the mountain of . . .

» Three-for-two packets of pregnancy tablets, which you got because you were scared of running out.

» Post-pregnancy pills (I read the side of the box, these are the same as the pregnancy ones).

» Breastfeeding tablets to make sure bubs is getting everything they need.

Plus, you need to start giving stuff to your baby: supplements, multivitamin liquids, Vitamin D drops. Luckily, these all come in one handy bottle these days and they are age specific.

But all the pill popping is worth it (I hope), as I need my hair and I'm sick of hangnails. I want to feel like I have energy again, and not like I'm dragging my arse around just going through the motions. If taking a handful of natural pills in the morning like candy will speed up the healing of my scar, help me to feed my child and allow me to function like the rest of humanity then sign me up and I will let others know what works and what doesn't. (On that note, turmeric, one of my candy pills, helps with energy, pain relief, blood flow and digestion.) When science and natural remedies have the answer, or at least seem to offer help, I will be a sucker and continue to buy into it. Long live the Mummy Mafia hotline that is constantly sharing its secrets. And, finally, thank you to my nail lady for my beautiful manicure. Having your nails done is also a remedy that I highly recommend.

I Can't Wait

Thanks to my profession as a nanny, my wee one was not my first baby, though she is my best baby, and she is mine. Even so, I could tell you in my sleep about all the milestones she's going to go through, and in what order, though that doesn't make them any less wonderful. Even though I've seen it all before, I still delight in her starting to point and wave, and then to talk and walk. Every first should be celebrated in the way it deserves to be. Back when I looked after babies for a living, I'd often get to witness a momentous moment, such as a baby taking their debut step, and then gently encourage the child to do it again for their parents.

But I digress. This blog is really a word of warning to everyone, me included, to slow down, take in the moments and allow yourself and your baby to let things happen in their own time. And this is more about you as a parent than it is about your baby, as regardless of what you've read about reaching milestones, it's important not to jump the gun. I've certainly made the mistake of saying, "I can't wait until . . . " I realised it was because I knew what was coming next and I was excited! And I have noticed other mums doing this, too, and we need to stop. It's putting pressure on our kids to perform, as we are always on the lookout to make sure we don't miss something. By doing this, we miss out on everything else in between. I'm kidding about the pressure on our kids bit by the way, but I'm not joking about missing the little things, those everyday wee gems and joys, as we wait with bated breath and our mental checklists for the big milestones.

In order to tackle my own problem with this, I started by changing my language. Instead of saying or thinking, "I can't wait . . .", I now say, "I am looking forward to . . ." This way, I am allowing myself to be excited about what's to come whilst still being present in every way for my baby right now. She is on the cusp of so many things and seems to be gaining new skills daily. For instance, the other day she decided to feed herself, rather ferociously, I might add. I have to sit on my hands as she independently throws food at herself and hopes to get it in via osmosis. She is also waving at everyone and anything, rolling and getting herself wedged under furniture. She stands thinking she can walk (though she can't and hasn't crawled yet), and during all of this, I have to adjust my brain and stop the expectations and the projections that I may put on her. And I have to say it is wonderful just to relax, be a new mum and get excited about watching my child take her own path and develop her own personality traits. I just love to see how she is getting on in the world, to watch her figure things out and to allow her to do it. She surprises and enthrals me, and when I'm with her, I forget what I know and relearn it with her.

The very fact that we are their mum means we are their number one fan at all times, and we couldn't be prouder when they have a lightbulb moment. But I for one need to let these happen organically and naturally and in bub's own time. I need to enjoy every day as a whole and be available to nothing happening at the same time as everything happening. So, I'm readjusting my timescales and this is helping me to relax into being a mum.

They say that on the day a baby is born, a mother is born. We are learning the world anew through them and I can't wait . . . no, I am looking forward to, the rest of this precious time we have together.

Things We Don't Say ...

Oh Mr Sun, Sun, Mr Golden Sun. Please shine down on me.

I have friends who sing this to their wee ones to get them to smile. And I'm pleased to say it works. But it also reflects how I am feeling. Writing this blog has been a long time coming, but being in the middle of the storm, I just couldn't do it. As much as I wanted to put fingers to keyboard, it was too hard. You see, I was under a black cloud. In my head it was always raining.

I suffer – and suffer is the right word – from postnatal anxiety. I didn't even know it was a thing until (in a fit of bravery) I mentioned my symptoms to a group of other mums, and one of them revealed that she not only suffers from the same condition, but she was enduring her second bout following the birth of her second child. She felt that I fit the profile. Postnatal depression seems to get all the attention, but there are other things out there to get you (and that's actually what the anxiety is about, as you worry about all the things that are going to get you and/or your baby). We just don't talk enough about it, so I'm going to try and change that. Here goes . . .

I'm nine months in and on the odd occasion, I still feel plagued by doubt and fear that I'm not bonding with my little one; that I'm failing her; that I don't talk enough to her; that I should be playing with her instead of having that cuppa. I am dropping feeds, too, due to being her chew toy – she is teething and chewing on my nipples instead of sucking on them, which is a sign she is weaning – and I've felt I've failed on that part of motherhood as well, as I wanted to do at least a year. I am going through physical as well as emotional changes, which in turn have probably brought out the anxiety in full force. Those feelings of inadequacy get blown up as you move from being your little one's world to no longer needed as much.

My anxiety manifests itself in such a way that when her dad offered to go shopping and take her with him, so I could have a little rest, I had an awful image that they would get into an accident and both die. I couldn't imagine living without them, so I decided that I couldn't let them go without me. Bubs is my life, and I'm constantly afraid that someone's going to take her from me. I have to switch over every TV programme about hospitals and kidnappings, or else I won't sleep. On a windy day, when she's in her pram, I have to hold on so tight, as I imagine it and her being blown away from me. These are just a few examples of how my anxious mind operates.

Those days when I'm crying inside and out at different points are crippling. I'm holding my baby so close and crumbling inside. What we don't talk about is how long this actually lasts for. In my head, I feel I should be over it, better, but I'm not. And that adds to the feeling of failure. I get down on myself for not only failing as a mother, but also as a person.

It's no wonder then that I fell headfirst into postnatal depression. I didn't want to go out, to get dressed or to bother with myself. Now, don't get me wrong, this never filtered down to my child. She was washed, fed, dressed and entertained. But when she was occupied by either sleeping or playing, I plunged into despair. Because I was feeling so useless and hopeless at being a mother, I reckoned I was constantly letting her down and that she'd be better off with anyone but me. Seemingly little things became huge problems in my head. For instance, I felt her meals should be tastier and not so repetitive. I decided her days should be fuller and that I should be playing games with her all of the time. I felt like a lazy mum, and as if I was doing the bare minimum. As a nanny, there was an expectation and pressure to be up to someone else's standards. But when left to my own devices, they slipped off the cliff, or at least that's how I saw it.

This sucks, it really does. When the cloud descends, it can be a struggle to breathe at times. You are crying inside all of the time, outside when you can and often in public. As I stare into the abyss, I can lose track of time, so minutes can feel like hours, and vice versa. I don't sleep, even when my baby is (I actually look forward to her waking in the night so I will feel a sense of purpose by nursing or resettling her) and I'm not interested in food, yet I can't stop eating. I'm not bouncing back (see food intake) to my pre-pregnancy weight, which leads me down the rabbit hole of feeling fat, frumpy and ugly, as I chastise myself for having no willpower. I'm overwhelmed and I can't admit that I'm not coping as I did when I was a nanny (deep down, I'm aware I know what I'm doing, as I am a highly qualified childcare practitioner). In a way, what makes it worse is that the despair only occurs periodically. If it was all the time, I could be brave enough to say I am suffering and get whatever help is out there. But it happens every so often. Sometimes for days, sometimes just for hours. For instance, it's a good day today, as I write this, and it's been that way for about a fortnight. But I don't know when this good spell will end or whether I may have come through to the other side.

Once, my husband said to me, "Honey, I think you have postnatal depression," so I obviously wasn't hiding it as well as I thought. All mothers – I'll let that sink in – *all* mothers suffer from this at some point in the first year of motherhood. During the first few months, the HV (Health Visitor) asked me to fill in a happiness questionnaire. But I was fine then. I had just had a baby and she was beautiful. I was surfing the oxytocin wave. It's only now, as I enter the last months of the first year, that I am starting to crash. But no one warned me. Again, ALL of us will experience one or two or all of the symptoms of PND at some point. It's kind of reassuring that we are all in this together, if you know what I mean. Others have survived and we will too.

There is help out there if you need it, medication and counselling, etc., but in addition, here are some ways to make your days sunnier, too. And I am trying them . . .

» **Get outside.** Rain or shine, fresh air is a life saver. Take some breaths, and I don't mean just in and out, take some

THE MOTHERLOAD - BLOGS FOR MUMMY

deep breaths and with your outward one, push out all of your negativity. Imagine your dark thoughts, vibes and feelings as poison to be expelled from your body.

» **Do something for yourself.** Go to the gym or get your nails done. I'm currently doing pilates, which is good for relaxation, fitness and company.

» **Talk to someone.** It could just be about the weather, or, if you're brave enough to admit that today isn't shaping up to be a great one, you may find that the person you're talking to has noticed you were down but didn't want to say anything, or they may know exactly how you're feeling. Partners can be good for providing a shoulder to cry on. Mine just let me cry . . . I didn't need to say anything, I just needed to let my emotions out.

» **Accept every invitation.** Other mums will be at different stages of PND, so when you're having a bad day, they will be having a good one. Inadvertently, they can pull you out of your slump.

» **Get organised.** You will feel a sense of achievement if you can get just one task in your day completed. There is a wonderful guide to doing that called *The Organised Mum Method* by Gemma Bray. It advises you to only do something for thirty minutes. So, in that half hour slot, rearrange the linen cupboard, book that holiday or write that blog you've been putting off. Setting a time limit on your activities will prevent you from feeling so overwhelmed by them.

» **Make a list.** Write down the things you need to do over the course of your day. For example, something as simple as 'eat breakfast' could be one of them. Then get on with your day and start crossing things off. When the clouds do crowd in and you feel like you are pinned down, distraction can be the key to pushing them aside. Heck, having a shower gets one thing off the list and hot water can be very healing. A bath works even better.

We have so much pressure put on us – by society and our own selves – it's no wonder we wobble here and there. We can easily become trapped under the weight of expectation. But it's OK not to be OK once in a while. We need to remember to give ourselves permission to stop, acknowledge that we are suffering, wallow in it, work through it and come out the other side. Let's allow positivity, optimism, support and good vibes to blow all the bad stuff away.

Therapy

Over the past year, I've been having a wee battle with my body, mentally, physically and emotionally. But today, a reprieve came in the most unexpected and wonderful way. Let me explain the battle. Physically, I am not bouncing back. This is my fault, as I have no willpower, so I'm feeling angry at myself. This is a life-long battle that rages on in every woman because of society and its pressures to conform to the norm. Motherhood just amplifies and piles on, literally, the pounds of expectation on top of what we were already labouring under before we went into labour. Mentally, I still have PTSD about the C-section and being coerced into something I did not want and wasn't ready for. Plus, my scar still hurts. According to the doctor who recently looked at it, I fall into the category of women for whom the nerves have been damaged, so that area will always be fizzy and painful to the touch, as the nerves misfire. In addition, the memory of being sliced open is something I'm still working on. And finally, emotionally, I'm still suffering from bouts of postnatal anxiety and depression, although this is improving as I learn to cope better.

With all this going on, today came as a surprise. I had therapy, and not the kind I probably should have undergone, given what I've just revealed. I had beauty therapy, and I can't recommend it enough to mothers who need to reclaim their sense of womanhood and their body. It's so weird, but until I had it, I didn't realise that it was exactly what I needed. So, here goes. Every mum knows that from the moment of conception, your body is a vessel and no longer belongs to you. You need to nourish the baby and allow them to grow and take everything they need from you. In addition, healthcare professionals claim your body, checking it and the baby by prodding you and sticking things on, in and around you. Your blood pressure is taken, you hand over samples of your urine and let them constantly test your blood sugar levels. At one point, I was doing the blood sugar prick test every three hours and emailing in the results. Then, when it's time to give birth, there are monitors and needles and other people's hands – lots of other people's hands – all over you (that was the catalyst for today's revelation, but I'll get to that). Once bubs is out, you have yet more people's hands moving you about and swapping around pads in your most intimate areas. There are people monitoring your bowels and bladder and sticking needles in you. Your body still belongs to your baby, as they need that skin-to-skin comfort, and when you're breastfeeding you learn quickly to just get on with it and to flop out your boobs regardless of other people's reactions.

But now I'm a year in and my body is once again my own. My baby has weaned completely, and she is becoming more independent and doesn't need holding so much. My hormones are returning to normal and I can no longer use the excuse that I have just had a baby – it's time to get fit and fab again, restore my core muscles and put on a bra. So, when my friends gave me a voucher to a spa, I had no idea (and I'm not sure they did, either) that it would be a revelation and provide me with such a healing moment. I indulged in a body brush, facial and head massage. I have had massages before, and although these were all before pregnancy, it meant I didn't expect it to have such an effect. After all, I wasn't exactly trying something new. But allowing another person to touch and caress me, be it with a wire brush, and for me to be pretty much naked except for a pair of panties that wouldn't stand up to a stiff wind (we all know the flimsy types they give you) was liberating, especially as she brushed my tummy. I felt all the old anxiety and emotional weight of allowing my body to be in the hands of a stranger wash away with the shower I had halfway through the treatment, before I was slathered in wonderful warm goop and had my aches and pains rubbed away.

The session allowed me to give my consent to being touched, which made me feel that I was reclaiming my body, especially my tummy area. By allowing it to be seen and viewed without judgement or an agenda left me with a feeling of peace. For those of you who know pain, be it in your head, heart or body, you'll get that you don't always know how much you're enduring until that pain is no longer there. And I'm so pleased to say that mine has gone and I feel light and free. I'm still vulnerable, but in a good way, if that makes sense.

It has been a journey for me, but I can't say this enough to mothers, after the first year of learning and living with your baby, find a sitter or ask your mother, auntie, sister or neighbour to help, someone you trust. Leave bubs with them and take some time for you. Then allow someone other than a healthcare professional or a loved one to touch and soothe your body. In other words, take a load off and give yourself a moment when you're not thinking about feeds, nappies and your lack of sleep at home. Be present in your mind and body and relax. This was a step to healing that I wanted, but although I knew I needed it, I had no idea how to actually achieve it. It came from other mothers and was perhaps inspired by their own experience. It was a gift, and I will cherish it as they gave me back to me. I suggest that everyone should go into therapy.

Mummy MOT

Following on from my PTSD (Post-traumatic stress disorder), which resulted from having a C-section, my PND (Postnatal depression), which lasted thirteen months, and my breakthrough moment of having my tummy brushed in a massage, I took some of my friends' advice and had a Mummy MOT. You see, having sorted out my mental and emotional stress, I now needed to get myself fixed physically. I am/was still experiencing tightness, numbness and pain around my surgery scar. I also had water retention, a lovely mummy pooch/shelf that would not shift and was suffering from incontinence.

That's the thing, we do get shy after we have had a baby, maybe because our body wasn't our own during pregnancy and every (qualified) Tom, Dick and Harry had a listen to and a touch of our tummies. Then we had to quickly get over whipping our boobs out whenever our baby needed them, meaning every (unqualified) Tom, Dick and Harry got a good look at them. Yes, our bodies made life and we are proud of that, but society does not make us proud of the aftermath, involving stretch marks, the aforementioned shelf under our belly buttons and the parts of us that sag. Additionally, we think the aches and pains are just part of motherhood, so we don't think to mention them. I was amazed by the response I received from other mums after I posted a simple status on my Facebook page about how great the MOT was. Mums admitted that they shared some of the same physical issues as me, even after many months. They said they had just learned to put up with them and didn't realise they could get help to fix them. We seem to have this 'mustn't grumble' approach and just get on with it.

I think we need to lose the shyness, stand up and look after ourselves. Trust me, it takes a bit of work, but you're worth it. Personally, I've hit upon doing Kegel exercises and having firm but gentle tummy massages to encourage the excess fluid to dissipate. I am one week into my new regimen, and I'm pleased to say that the bump has gone down and coughing and sneezing is no longer so daunting. We don't have to put up with this stuff anymore, there are professionals willing to actually help us – hallelujah. Other mums I have spoken to have had their hips readjusted so they can walk again without pain or clicking, their uterus put back into place (it's a thing and more common than you'd think), trapped nerves soothed, rips and tears sorted out and the big one – Diastasis Recti (abdominal separation) – reversed. This is where the tummy muscles are stretched so much during pregnancy that they don't come back together and leave a dip. It's very common yet not really known or talked about.

It makes perfect sense that we should have a check-up after giving birth, especially if we intend to go again. We need a bit of a service and a tune up; a bit like a car getting road ready after being driven off a cliff. I can't promise that there is a person in your area who will be able to assist, but there will be somewhere, and it's well worth the appointment, even if it's just to be reassured that you're not going crazy and that it is normal to have to hold it in when you go over a bump in the road, and yes, your pooch will go away if you work on it. Now, if I could only put down the chocolate and lose that wee tipple every night to help it along further. . .

The M Word

I was pretty smug. I had read that it only happens in the first few months of breastfeeding, and as my little one is nine months old, I thought I'd dodged a bullet. But I was wrong. And BOY, it hurts like hell, and I now know you can get it at any time while you're breastfeeding (or even not), especially when the little one is self-weaning.

I'm talking about mastitis, which is the inflammation of one or more of the mammary glands within the breast. It can be felt as a hard, sore spot and can be caused by an infection in the breast or by a plugged milk duct.

I got it over the Easter period. I was feverish, in pain, nauseous and my head was pounding. In short, I felt like I had been punched in the left breast by Mike Tyson. I had never known pain like it. My boob was hot, hard and constantly throbbed. No amount of hot showers, massaging or feeding my baby could shift it. It was time to a) Google it and b) reach out to the Mummy Mafia. Both came through for me. As a result of what I discovered through them, here is my advice:

» **Call your doctor.** If your surgery is anything like mine, you need a crystal ball to know when you're going to be sick, as they book appointments that far in advance, but I managed to get an emergency call back from a duty doc and they immediately gave me a prescription for antibiotics.

» **Go shopping for one of your five-a-day.** Cabbage, to be precise. Grab a couple of those big leaves and make yourself a new bra with them. I know it sounds weird, and I am not sure of the science behind it, but boy does it work. I cooked a couple of those suckers for a few days with my body heat. They do smell, but I was in such pain that I didn't care. And you do get funny looks. This was especially the case when

161

I went to the dentist and noticed they were peeking out of my bra half-way through my check-up.

» **Hot water of any kind will provide relief.** Get in the shower or run a hot bath and knead the affected breast under the water to move the blockage. For me, it hurt just to touch the breast, let alone the blockage, but I had to keep treating it. A hot water bottle down your bra (or tucked into your cabbage leaf) also helps.

» **Charge up your electric toothbrush.** You have to move the milk, and a gentle massage of the area using the vibration of the toothbrush will help. Start on the outer rim of the breast and massage towards the blockage and then to your nipple to move the milk downwards and out.

» **Chin to breast.** We naturally do this anyway, but the idea is to focus on the area of the blockage and, while bubs is feeding, to manoeuvre and squish the breast towards your chin to try and shift the lump.

» **Oil up.** Massaging body oil into your breast will help you to get your fingers into the deep tissue. Alternatively, drag a large-toothed comb down the affected breast. Both of these techniques can aid the movement of the milk to the nipple, where it can flow out.

» **Pump and dump.** Use your hand or a breast pump. This can be good for the baby, too, as if it turns out to be an infection, the milk will taste funny to them. I felt like a cow at milking time and had to turn up the TV to drown out the sound of my electric pump.

» **Feed your baby often.** I had an infection, which meant bubs was skipping her feeds, so encouraging her to help Mummy out wasn't easy. But she did her best and was obliging as I twisted her around into every position: holding her like a rugby ball, dangling over her and even sitting her up on my knee. Trying different positions helps to drain and refill different ducts and, hopefully, the release of new milk will push the residue through and let it all flow away.

» **Painkillers.** I was in agony and the pills only just took the edge off, but I had to take them, as even carrying the wee one on the affected side was hard going. Don't be brave, take the medicine.

Once I had got on top of it, numerous mums I mentioned the issue to said how much it hurt. It's something that anyone can get at any time, whether that's early on in breastfeeding and/or when they start easing off on the feeds. You can get it repeatedly (fingers crossed that doesn't happen to me, as once was definitely enough, thank you), in both breasts and even when you're not even breastfeeding. So, ladies who are on the bottle, get educated, too, just in case.

I hope that you never experience mastitis, as it's something I wouldn't wish on my worst enemy. But if you do join the club, at least you now know what to do.

Push Me, Pull Me

It starts as I am sitting on the couch, three maybe four episodes into a boxset, with the wee one asleep in my arms. The voice inside my head tells me I can't just sit here; it says I should be doing something constructive, such as the laundry, the cleaning, having a shower, etc, etc. And I start to feel guilty about not doing those things. Then the other voice starts, the one the first calls the 'lazy voice'. It asks, "Why?" and tells me that with the exception of the shower, all the other stuff can wait. It's not as if I'm neglecting my child. She is in my arms and I'm bonding with her. "Oh, but she needs to learn to sleep in her cot, not on you," the first voice says. "But she already sleeps through the night," says the second. "What's the problem?"

I tend to agree with the 'lazy' voice. There's plenty of time to implement routines and schedules and be mindful of when and where they sleep. Besides, I do adhere to night and day sleep rules. (Day sleep is in a brightish room, with loud noises and in a pushchair or a day bed. Night sleep is in a dark room, with hushed tones and in a cot, a bed bag or under blankets.) Even so, the voices in my head are usually having a full-on row by this point. I ask myself why we are made to feel guilty or unproductive during the day. It took time to grow this person – mine is only three months old – and just as my body isn't expected to physically bounce back to its pre-pregnancy state, nor should my energy levels. I am breastfeeding, which means I also need to eat and drink a lot. It's draining, on every part of me. Yes, it's true that you're resting when feeding, but it's still a job. Just because you sit behind a desk to work doesn't mean that it constitutes a rest!

I read a wonderful article recently about mother's rest time, which argued that holding a sleeping bubs and simply swimming around in the love hormones is good for us. It brings balance and peace to an overworked mind and body. So, why do I still have an internal argument every day? Well, it's because we are too hard on ourselves. As mums, we overthink things and try to be everything to everyone. We still need to maintain our relationships with the other people in our lives, be it husbands/partners, our other children and our friends, when all we really want to do is sleep. We still need to complete all the jobs we did before, be they unpaid or paid after our maternity leave comes to an end. The house still needs to be looked after and we still need to eat, pay the bills and try to leave the house, all while looking after another human's every need. And we yell at ourselves for not keeping all those balls in the air. Well, I do. Another mother put it in perspective for me. She is further down the line with an older one, and she said to me how she used to hate the hour-long feeds on the couch because she felt tied there when she could be using the time more wisely. Now with an 18-month-old who doesn't sit down, she would give anything to have that 'forced time' back again. But note how she still used the term 'forced time'. Why is feeding them and then letting them settle on you while enjoying their mummy mattress 'forced' time? Where else do you need to be? Statistically, parents have already spent more than half their allotted time (going on averages) with their children by the time they are eleven. That's it. Before they even reach their teenage years that quality time together is already ebbing away. My dad summed it up when he remarked how you spend the first couple of years being chased by your kids for attention and the rest of your years chasing them for attention. He has been listening to the song *Father and Son* by Yusuf/Cat Stevens, which perfectly sums up the limited time we have with each other as a family.

What I'm trying to say here is to hear the voice out. If the matter is pressing, such as you have no clean clothes or food in the house and you really do smell or could cook chips off your hair, then pop bubs down, get off the couch and get on with your errands. But if not, then don't sweat it, because your rest time, with bubs or without, is important for your mind, body and soul. They don't say "sleep when they do" for nothing! You need to look after yourself, too. Like the air crew say during the safety briefing before take-off, put on your own mask before helping others.

I think I will have those competing voices in my head forever, because society dictates that women can do everything. It has that wrong by the way; we can do anything, not everything! Although I will continue to argue with myself daily, I'm hoping the boxset bonding voice wins, not because I'm lazy, but because time with your child goes too quickly, and you only notice that when it's gone. So, follow my advice and find a comfy spot. Ensure you have a drink, a snack, your phone, your TV remote, a blanket, a muslin and a dummy close to hand. Now pick up bubs and relax.

More TMI, Please

Just when you think you are rolling along and on top of this thing called motherhood, another twist of the rollercoaster looms, which is in fact when it's time to get off the ride that is breastfeeding. Those breastfeeding hormones – the ones you had got used to and could deal with – take a turn, and a rather sinister one at that. You see, what no one tells you is that when you want to get off, your body doesn't take it very well. I had to find out in a baby music class, from another mother, who just happened to drop it into the conversation. And that moment of what could be deemed as 'over sharing' actually saved my mental health! Our mums, HVs (Home Visitors), midwives, etc., really are useless at sharing. Do you think you are going to scare us off beforehand? Did you forget? Where is the leaflet on this? Why was I not warned? Why was my family not warned?!!

I had been feeling deranged. I mean, my husband's breathing was annoying when I was pregnant, but this was on another level. It makes sense, ladies, that when your body is ramping up to feed your child, your hormones go into overdrive to push the body to produce the milk. It's logical, I know, and it does make sense, therefore, that when your baby is not taking as much, those same hormones power down to help the body cope. I'm happy that my body is coping, but it seems my mind was not let into this little pow wow!

So, when someone casually mentioned to me that when your baby goes onto solids and they start dropping feeds, your hormones go crazy, a wave did roll over me. It was a relief to know that it was OK, it was normal and that my children and, more importantly, my husband could come out of the storm shelter. But a heads up would have been nice. Mums are pressured, to say the least, to get on the breastfeeding bandwagon, but what we are not told is how the hell to get off it, or that it's a bumpy ride, just as much as it was to get on. Those words "it will happen naturally" and "transition" get batted about (breastfeeding mums, hands up how many times have you wanted to smack the next person who said that to you when you were starting this journey?), but no one, and I mean no one, mentions how crap you will feel emotionally, sometimes mentally and also physically when your journey is ending. Bubs has taken to solids like a duck to water and is dropping feeds left, right and centre. And that is OK, and I'm happy for her. But we as women need to share the knowledge that we gain from this episode of new motherhood. Just like breastfeeding, weaning will hurt a lot to begin with, and for a good wee while. You will not (most likely) get it straight away. It can take months to achieve. Your milk will not be enough at times and pour from your body at others. And when the journey ends, the surges and withdrawal of mother milk and mummy hormones will fluctuate like a motherf**ker!

So, it turns out I'm not going nuts (well, that's up for debate), I was just misinformed, or not informed at all. We need to share, speak up and tell others – just in case. In other words, we need to give Too Much Information (TMI), because there is no such thing as TMI when it comes to parenting and knowing your body, your mind and your emotions. I was saved via a snippet of someone else's experience, and I hope that you will in turn understand that you're not going crazy if this happens to you too.

Things I'm Learning (Five Months Before, Five Months After)

After years, and I mean years, of longing, it finally happened, and the universe chose me to be a mum. I had many friends who were already in the club, and they were all rooting for me, while comparing notes and filling me in on the joys of motherhood. But when I asked them about pregnancy, they were uncharacteristically unforthcoming. And now I know why. It sucks!

Right now, I am only five months in, but I'll give it to you straight. While I knew it wasn't going to be an easy ride, I had no idea it was going to be this hard. Right off the bat, I was constantly either being sick or feeling nauseous. In order to get you prepared, I thought I'd document what I've learned so far in my pregnancy. This is the *before*.*

*Just to balance things out a little, I've also included an update of what I've learned in the five months *after* giving birth.

Before:

Sickness. Whoever coined the term morning sickness can go and take a flying leap; it's morning, lunch, dinner and night-time sickness; it's weeing yourself while you throw up, and retching and projectile vomiting out of a car window; it's any and every smell setting you off, no matter how much you loved those aromas before. I didn't drink that much coffee in my pre-pregnancy life, but I found the smell welcoming and warm. Now I run from the room whenever my other half so much as puts on the kettle.

Aches and pains. You get these funny and strange ones in places that you weren't even aware of before. And no other book will tell you this. During my first meeting with the midwife, it was she who confirmed that the sharp aches and pains I was feeling in the vicinity of my abdomen were just my womb stretching and, therefore, nothing to worry about.

Fatigue. The tiredness washes over you at strange moments, and I've developed the ability to fall asleep at anytime and anywhere. While pregnant, my sister once dropped off on London Bridge! As for me, I took a 'power nap' in my dentist's waiting room.

Soreness. My breasts are so tender it feels like I'm growing rocks instead of milk ducts. I haven't worn a bra for ninety per cent of my pregnancy so far. I can put on a crop top for support, but that's as far as I'll go.

Loose teeth. I feel like they are all going to fall out, which makes eating hard because I'm afraid one might actually drop on my plate during dinner. This is due to pregnancy hormones causing the ligaments and bones in my mouth to loosen. I've been reassured that this won't actually cause tooth loss, and that it's temporary.

Acid. If throwing up wasn't enough, then comes the indigestion, heartburn and reflux, which strikes day or night and whether I am sitting or lying down. I have known pregnant women to walk around with straws so they can suck up antacid medicine whenever it strikes. I find that fizzy sweets and apple cider vinegar also help.

Hormones. All I can say is get ready for a rollercoaster ride, ladies. You'll want to rip someone's head off just for breathing the wrong way one minute, then feel the urge to cuddle them to death the next. Oh, and don't watch TV ads, they'll make you cry.

Clit kicks. Yes, this is exactly what it sounds like. When bubs is running out of room in there and starts pushing around, you'll get kicks and punches to organs you never even knew you could feel. And the worst is the thump to the bladder and the kick to the nerve that leads to the clitoris. It's like an electric shock affecting the whole of your nether regions. Prepare to cry out and make a funny face, but not out of ecstasy!

I now know why, when I told my female friends who are mothers that I wanted to savour every moment of my pregnancy, they just said "best of luck with that!" I should have known something was up by their lacklustre response. Maybe that's why they call it "keeping mum!"

After:

No one gets their birth plan. If you are lucky to get a semblance of it, keep it to yourself, because the rest of us didn't. Women can vary between feeling sad and resentful over this. We mostly want to slap the next person who says, "Well, at least you have a happy and healthy baby." My advice regarding having a birth plan is to lower your expectations and just plan to give birth.

You will bleed a lot. No matter how bubs came into the world, your body has to get rid of all that fluid, and it takes its goddamn time doing it. Most of the mums I've spoken to have asked their home visitor whether they should still be bleeding so much after five or six weeks. At one point, I thought my periods had started up again or that I'd popped a stitch. But it is normal, and when you know you're going to bleed for that long you'll feel better about it happening.

Having a baby is painful. During pregnancy, I experienced aches and pains in places I never knew I had; post-baby, I'm not feeling much at all. This is due to being numb from my belly button to my pubic bone. It's a wee side-effect of surgery that can take years to fizzle out. Other mums experience rips and tears, inside and out, which take time to heal. It can be quite a while, and for some a bit of an ordeal, before your body reverts back to its pre-pregnancy state (though it never quite goes back to normal).

Whether it's via breast or bottle, feeding is a bitch. Both have their pros and cons. With breast, the milk is readymade and no sterilisation is required. It's all on tap and to temperature. The cons are leakage, sore nipples and an occasional limited supply. It can hurt at times and you also get blockages. The pros of bottle feeding are that the formula is easy to make up, you can see exactly how much they are getting, and others can help with the feeds. However, it's a pain lugging the bottles around and having to clean them, etc. When it comes to choosing what to do, there are no easy answers.

At the beginning, none of us know what we are doing. Some of us just fake it better. So, don't worry if yours isn't sleeping, eating and pooping at the times and at the frequency you thought they would. Motherhood is not a pyramid scheme; instead, we support each other like a rope bridge, all linked and held together through many strands and things in common, while trying to make it across the chasm that is parenthood.

More hormones. These tricky little fuckers sneak up on you and infiltrate all, and I mean all, areas of your life. It does slow down after a while, but after five months, I still have duvet days when I can't stop crying. Or I feel like I'm failing my baby, my partner, my family or society in some way. Yesterday, I was sad simply because we were so busy that I felt I had not spent enough time staring at her.

No matter how much laundry, dishes, cleaning, etc., you do, there will always be more. But you're not getting any younger and, more importantly, neither is your baby, so leave it and spend time with them. Rest well and claim some time for yourself without your baby if you need to, even if that means taking a shower when you don't need one. If you've had a stressful day, then put on that box set and chill. A happy mummy equals a happy baby, and vice versa. Hand them to someone else for a while. There is nothing like hearing them giggle from another room.

Other mothers, no matter what age they are, be they grandmothers, mothers, mothers-in-law, friends or ladies in the street are the best support network you will ever have. They are there to offer a kind word, a knowing smile, a coffee or a night out. Often, a bit of time spent with other mums is all we need to get through the day. Don't get me wrong, dads are great, but nothing beats girlfriends and other mothers.

Routine Adaptations

Just as the stories you read to your little one are adaptations of the original tale, the story of your family life can also be tweaked. It's an adaptation of the original *and* of the fantasy. We all had dreams about how we wanted it to go, or, in my case, how it *would* go based on my prior experience as a nanny. We all had to shift and move and adapt to how it actually is. What I am so vaguely talking about here is that hush hush word *'routine'*.

It's screamed at you from the baby books, mentioned in passing by older generations of mothers who did it one way or another, and spoken of in faint tones at breastfeeding and playgroups. It's a scary word for mums, as it signifies pressure and expectation, failure and fault. In short, it sucks. But I'm here to tell you that you are looking at it all wrong. Routine is a good thing, but just like the fairytales that we read aloud over and over again, it needs to be adapted for your family.

Routine is something that you can fall back on, and it should be helpful rather than regimented. I'll give you an example from a recent conversation I had with a nanny I know. She asked me when my wee one slept. I told her it was whenever she can, as my days are different every week. Therefore, we pop her down for a snooze here and there, depending on the day and the place and the mode of transport we are using. I lamented that when I was a nanny, sleep times were the same every day, according to the stage my charges were at. For example, when they were small it was every couple of hours, which went to twice a day when they got older. Now as a mum, that kind of routine has gone out of the window. This is for two reasons. In London, classes were available every day and at all times of the day, so you could pick and choose ones to suit your schedule. We don't have that where I now live in Northern Ireland. Also, classes and playdates were local, so you could walk to them (and schedule in a stroller nap), whereas here I have to drive to most places. I have to work with what I've got, so some days she takes her naps in the car, some days in her stroller and some days in the house. Sometimes, it's a mixture of all three. Despite the disparity, when I looked over our week, I saw that my schedule had a pattern and that bub's routine was a weekly one rather than a daily one. I had adapted her schedule to fit around our life. In other words, I had changed the script,

Quite by accident, we had fallen into a schedule and an expectation of what each day would bring. And it worked for us. So, when you're having a rare moment of peace, try to sit back and mentally run through your week. See if there's a pattern to the madness and, if so, that's your routine. It should work for you and, most importantly, your child. They need things to be roughly the same and to know what's coming next, even if that's on a weekly rather than a daily or hourly basis. So, if you keep some things the same, such as the accessories they go to sleep with (for bubs it's her dummy and a muslin) and the time they have a class or a regular playdate, they'll get to know the rhythm of family life. You can then fall back on this when needed. For example, when you've arrived home after a holiday, you can still put them down for a sleep at the time – ish – when they'd usually go down for a nap. Your mum brain knows what to do even when you are mainlining coffee just to get through the day. Your routine can be a comfort for all involved.

Something you will encounter quite early on with the wee one is The Witching Hour, or, as I call it, The Bitching Hour (if only it was for just an hour!). This term was coined by mummies to explain that time in the evening when bubs fusses, for no reason at all, as if they are simply trying to keep you on your toes. What helped yesterday doesn't today and what does today won't tomorrow. It's usually after The Golden Hour, which is that time when they are happy, full, gurgling away, kicking on their mats or on the couch and being so generally gorgeous that you think, "Oh, I've got this parenting thing down." Then everything turns. They cry, wriggle and want to either be put down or picked up. They are either too hot or too cold, their nappy may be slightly wet and uncomfortable, so they want it off, or they may have a trapped air bubble, i.e. a burp that just needs to be teased out with some gentle patting, etc. (Please note that this is different from trapped wind or a sore tummy, which requires the firm massaging of the tummy/bowel area.) The light is off, the TV is too loud, the light is on, they want a cuddle or their dummy or they don't want a cuddle or their dummy. I am literally just running through the things my daughter has complained about over the past few weeks, and she is only two months old. But never fear, there is good news and there is bad news. The good is that this is completely normal and nothing to worry about. New mums do get a bit apprehensive, as the words colic and reflux can get flung around, usually by in-laws and partners, who don't know any more than you do. This is the time to trust yourself. If something were wrong, you would feel it. The bad news is that there's no cure for them fussing. It's just a phase (you will get to know this term, as everything in a baby's life is 'just a phase') that you both just have to get through. As I've said, what worked one day might not the next, and then suddenly you're out of the phase and into the next one – there is always a next one. But don't despair, there are tricks that you can use, and routine is one of them.

As I've explained, this can be a loose one, but remember that babies look to you to understand when and where they are going to do something. I listen to them to find out what they want and then reinforce their choices. Your job is to insert other things between their cues that tell you they want to sleep and eat, etc. So, develop a pre-bathtime routine or sit on the couch and watch a certain TV programme with them, etc. The Witching Hours will become shorter and less frequent, as they start to expect things to happen. They will know to look forward to bathtime and to the sound of the *EastEnders* theme tune (as it'll mean snuggling with you on the couch for a while). Children are like rivers, you can't stop their flow, but you can divert them.

As I've touched upon, this story belongs to you and your child. It's not the same for each family or each child, rather it's based on a story you heard somewhere, before drawing on bits from other stories and making your own version. It's also ever changing, as new threads, characters and plot twists occur. Sometimes, it flows really well, and at other times it's darn scary, but just like in a book, chapters come to an end and the story moves on, leaving room for new adventures to begin. So, don't panic upon hearing the words 'routine' and 'schedule'. See them as a guide to discovering what is best for you and your child. Most importantly, if your routine isn't working for you then change it. Trust me, there are no judgements amongst mums and no set rules. Throw the script in the bin if you need to and start over. We are all in this together, so if they need to sleep here or there or at this time and not the other then let them. If you're doing something that is no longer working for you, such as taking them into your bed, then stop, reassess things and change tack. It will take a few weeks to learn the new rhythm, but children adapt (and faster than you might think). Routine is all about adjusting to your surroundings and discovering what does and doesn't work. Just remember to make the chapter your own. Take out bits, rewrite others and don't feel the need to justify it to anyone, especially yourself. It's your routine, so own it.

Ode to the Midnight Mum

So, I saw in 3.50 am this morning. And as I rocked a very frustrated wee one in the milky light of a streetlamp, I wrote this blog in my head. Bubs had woken up, got pissed off she was awake and proceeded to have a full-on tantrum in her cot. Nothing, and I mean nothing, could sway her from venting her frustrations. It was hard to watch and listen to, but she did not want to be held or touched or given a drink of water, a dummy or a muslin. She was writhing around, kicking out and thrashing the sleep bag. And I had to let it happen and wait. It lasted for what seemed like forever, which was probably five minutes, and then she allowed me to pick her up and she settled in my arms. She did not sleep, no, I wasn't that lucky, but she was accepting visitors, so I sat and rocked her. Of course, I was just in thin pjs, with no slippers on, and she was all cosy in her sleep bag, so you can guess who got cold first. I grabbed a blanket and tried as best I could to cover all extremities, hers and mine. That's when I thought of the midnight massive, or the midnight masses, who were no doubt wide awake, too.

At times, us mums function on less sleep than torture victims. Perhaps I've watched too many American TV soldier programmes, but sometimes it feels as if someone is trying to extract information out of me. Believe me, I would give away all my secrets for a few extra minutes of kip. But the other thing that occurred to me is that apart from the fact I would have liked us both to have been asleep – I say both because when she is up, I am up, as the invisible cord that still attaches us is very much in operation and I can't sleep if she's restless – I wouldn't have wanted to be anywhere else. I sat with her in the half-lit room, her head upon my chest, just taking in the moment and feeling her hair and warm head against my chin, her breath on my skin and her little fingers holding my hand, and I knew to take a mental snapshot. She will never be this small again. Yes, there will be other nights that I will get to hold her like this, but eventually one night will be the last and she will be bigger, older and not so in need of me in that way. I'm hoping it'll be when she's about 18.

It occurred to me that there will be a last time for everything. The last story I read to her, the last bathtime before I'm told to get out, the last rocking chair moment before we both won't fit in the seat together. Right now, the last breastfeed is approaching, and I am acutely aware of things falling away. So, even though I am up at four in the morning, I relish it, acknowledge it and bank it. I know that some of you are very sleep deprived and that you might have lost your enjoyment factor, but I want you to try and take in this wonderful moment at least once. Rest assured, it will stop soon (never too soon for some) and the next set of markers will come up. That's the other thing about motherhood, you just get over one set of hurdles or a challenge and a whole new set present themselves. As a mum of teenagers, too, I can tell you that the day will come when you can't get them out of bed!

Even though we are in separate houses, rooms and PJs, I salute the Midnight Mums (and Dads) of this world, who diligently get up every time, pace the floor for as long as it takes, rock and jiggle until their arms want to fall off and freeze (me this morning), all in the name of love. You are doing a good job, you've got this, and it will pass, just don't forget to remember these moments. x

Mother's Day

I am eight months into my life sentence, and this is my first review – Mother's Day. I guess we have two reviews a year; this day and their birthday. These days are a chance to check in and see how you are doing. Their birthday is the day to celebrate that you have kept them alive for another year. Contrary to what people may think, it's your moment as well as theirs. They may get the party, but you get the glee – woohoo, we did it! But Mother's Day is when everyone else gets to review you, I mean celebrate you. Woohoo, you did it!

As I've already said, this is my first Mother's Day and I'm so excited. She may not yet be big enough to make me anything that I will treasure forever, or to bring me watery tea and burnt toast in bed, but I am so thrilled to be here. So, my other half better get something from her to me, hint hint. Over the years, I have witnessed these occasions from the sidelines, crafting trinkets and pressing their feet and hands into paint to make plates and cards, before stepping aside to let Mum enjoy it all. This year, I'm front and centre! Even though some might say Mother's Day is just a commercial way of getting people to part with their money, right now I am new to the club and ready to receive my membership card. My daughter was so hard fought for that at times I never thought I would be here. I was always the bridesmaid never the bride.

Yes, every day is Mother's Day (and Father's Day) and we get the rewards all the time. But it's nice to have a day when what we do is brought under the spotlight. Mums are the silent warriors behind the scenes, the midnight zombies, the cleaner uppers after the meal, the ones that quietly and quickly throw together a playdate, World Book Day costume or arrange a sleepover at a moment's notice. We are the ones that wipe noses (and sometimes bottoms) that run like taps while feeling like death warmed up ourselves. We kiss booboos better and plaster scrapes. We brush hair and teeth and clean up dirt. Most of the time we know where that lost item of clothing is, or the keys or the cat. We work twenty-four-seven unpaid, sometimes unnoticed. There is no break or let up. We are literally on call day and night. We eat, shower, sleep and pee only if there is time and if our children allow us to, and even then we have company for some of it! There are millions of us unpaid workers around the world. Today, I saw a post saying that on average, mums get up at 6 am and work straight through to 10 pm. That's a sixteen-hour day, nearly a two-day working week in one, every day, including weekends. So, if a card company wants people to spend some cash on a mum then I say let them. We need to be seen and thanked. Just don't tell them that we would not have it any other way. (Heck, on second thoughts, tell them that we should get paid!) I say to all of you, Happy Mother's Day – you have earned it, you're doing great and you've got this. x

First Birthday, YOU made it!

My wee one is now well and truly into her toddling year, but with the attitude and foot stamping I'm frequently on the receiving end of, I'd say she's 13 months going on 21. And when this time is over, it's these little acts we'll forget, until we see another wee one doing them, and our heads and hearts will travel right back.

On holiday recently, my hubby and I had a minute to breathe and started to reminisce about the busy year that had just seemed to fly by. If you think about it, so much happens in their first year. There's being born for one, and then there's smiling, sitting, rolling, crawling, walking, talking, feeding and playing. It's a whirlwind, so here are a few ideas to ensure that everything doesn't just melt into the haze that was your first year together.

Do a book. I was given one of those well-meaning books that are designed for documenting all the firsts, etc. But I'm not very organised and quite honestly, I could not be arsed. When I had a moment in the evening, I sat my bum on the couch and vegged. However, you don't necessarily need to follow my example, as doing a book is a lovely way to document their pre- and post-birth lives (with some of these books, you get to add in pregnancy stuff, such as ultrasounds and any names you thought of, etc.).

Write a letter. This was something that my dad did for my sister and me on our birthdays. There were no personal computers back then (I'm that old), but at the risk of sounding old fashioned, I kind of like the idea of this letter being handwritten. In ours, Dad would tell us about our year; what had happened in the wider world and what had happened in ours, such as learning to walk, getting the hang of using a knife and fork or falling over and hurting ourselves, etc. He covered the little details that we wouldn't remember and that he would no doubt forget in time, too. He also told us how he felt about us, and about his hopes and dreams for our coming year and our future lives. When we were 21, he presented all these letters to us. It was such a wonderful and personal present, which I still treasure. I can't recommend this method enough.

Alternatively, now that we have the technology, you could **write an email.** We are always on the computer, so why not set up a domain name or email address for your child? They can always use it later in life, but until they get tech savvy, write them a message whenever they do something cool. And/or whenever you go on holiday together, send them photos and thoughts, memes and screenshots. Compose a quick email on the day they take their first steps or when their first tooth comes through. It'll already be time stamped, which will take away the hassle of one day trying to remember when these things occurred. You could also write a yearly summary, just like my dad did. Then, when it's time, they'll have a ready-made time capsule of their early lives.

Have a keepsake box. You can pop in the wee things that are important, such as the baby's hospital bracelet, their first birthday cards and their handprints in paint or plaster, etc. You might also want to keep the tiny socks and babygrows from their first days. I keep my box in the wardrobe and, as the things she's outgrown come through the wash, they get popped in there. I also throw in her artwork, Mother's and Father's Day cards, Christmas photos and first teeth, but you can put in whatever you hold dear. When the box fills up, tie it up with a ribbon and get another one. When they are older, it's wonderful for them to be able to touch their old things and be told the living history of their life. As they grow, school reports and any medals and certificates can be thrown into the mix. When it comes to the insurmountable art that will come your way, my suggestion is to be picky. Pick out a few choice pieces so that you can follow their progress, but you can't be expected to keep every pasta picture and stick person . . .

Make a keepsake item. Unless you are great with a needle and thread, you can always get someone else to do this for you. There are so many options and services that will turn those few items of baby clothing you have kept into something that can be displayed or used, such as a quilt. You can also get things like their coming-home outfit mounted and framed, along with their date of birth and birth weight. You could have a movie made containing the clips of their early years, or weave together treasured photos in one digital space. Whatever you decide to do, there will be a professional service available that will help you make sense of the chaos you have collated.

Open a bank account in your child's name. Kids have so much these days, and with the wonderful recycling, reusing and rehoming scheme that us mummies employ, our kids don't really want for much. So, why not ask your friends and family to give them money for their birthday or at Christmas? This would make a good alternative to a toy, particularly when they are too young to unwrap presents (often, they just want to eat the paper rather than see what the gift is anyway!). You could put the money towards more expensive items that come up every so often, such as a climbing frame or a bike. Or it might help to pay for a set of swimming lessons. Alternatively, save it all for when they are older. Shop around for the best interest rate and keep the cash turning over for when they are older and the big-ticket items, such as a car, university fees or a round-the-world adventure can be taken care of.

Whatever you decide to do, preserving your baby's first years is quick, easy and painless. You'll be glad you took the time, especially because when other children come along, life gets in the way and memories can fade. Both your later self and your child will thank you for doing it, though maybe not if you pull your memory box out at their 21st birthday party and show their friends that nude photo of them peeing on the lawn! Generally, however, they will be happy you took the time to honour them.

Drawing Your Own Conclusions

So, that was my first year (ish, see what I did there . . .). There have been highs and lows and ups and downs, and that was just me. My daughter seems to have thrived and flourished through my tried and tested methods of bringing up a baby unscathed. We are now onto Year Two.

I hope that you have gained something from this book: an idea or a light-bulb moment, a shared experience that you can use or file away, or perhaps just the reassurance that you're doing great and that you're not alone.

If you did like my blog offerings, there are plenty more that didn't make the final cut within these pages. I have popped them on the accompanying website to the book – www.allthesmallthingsbook. com.

Come and say hi, leave a comment or ask a question. If you liked my book, then please tell a friend about it and/or leave me a review on Amazon.

As I have said before, we are all in this together, so begin your cyber village with me. I'm still learning, practising and refining my mothering skills. I may know what's coming with my wee one, but I am still surprised every day by her. And I will share everything I discover with you . . .

Acknowledgements

This is the bit where I feel like I am an award winner . . . do I gush, thank my primary school teacher and everyone who believed in me? Well, yes, I kind of do . . . maybe not the primary school teacher, even though I do think of them fondly, it's more the other people who believed in me that I need to name and shame . . . I mean thank. They have listened, supported, encouraged. They have read, reread, spell checked and rejigged and they have provided countless opinions (some taken, some ignored) and shared with me their parenting experiences, their successes and failures and their struggles and highs.

I'd like to thank the wonderful Danielle and her team at Wrate's Editing Services, who made this dream a reality and helped me to find my voice inside my million scribbled ideas.

My gratitude also goes to my nearest and dearest, who went on this journey with me; my parents and especially my sister, who was my inspiration and who (along with other new mothers I've encountered over the years) got a bit lost with her first child and through many long days and longer nights put my advice into practice. This is how The Ish Plan was born, from helping my sister to relax and enjoy motherhood some thirteen years ago.

I want to thank my lucky seven ladies; we have been sounding boards for each other throughout our journeys of motherhood. We have known each other since we were fourteen and thought we knew it all!

I owe much to the Irish Daisy Ladies, with whom I went through my own journey of motherhood, often in the wee early hours of the morning.

I need to thank D, who gave me the love and encouragement to go for it and share this book with you.

To my kids, Kiss Kiss, Jojo and Busy, who were the guinea pigs in my career, and who all turned out OK in the end . . . kidding, I'm so proud of you!

And of course, to Aoife, who is my heart and my reason for living and laughing every day.